Christmas 2008

GRACE

FOR THE MOMENT®

VOLUME II

*More Inspirational
Thoughts for Each Day
of the Year*

Max Lucado

Published by J Countryman, a Division of Thomas Nelson, Inc., P.O. Box 141000, Nashville, Tennessee 37214.

Grace for the Moment® is a registered trademark of the J Countryman division of Thomas Nelson, Inc. and is registered in the U.S. Patent and Trademark office.

Compiled and edited by Terri Gibbs

Editorial supervision: Karen Hill, Administrative Editor for Max Lucado

ISBN 1-40410-097-0

www.thomasnelson.com
www.jcountryman.com

Designed by The DesignWorks Group; cover, David Uttley; interior, Robin Black
Photography by Steve Gardner, PixelWorks Studios, www.shootPW.com

Printed and bound in Belgium

PREFACE

My daughters have long since stopped doing this, but there was a time when they celebrated my daily arrival. Jenna was five years old, Andrea three. Denalyn would alert them, and they would scamper to the window, pressing noses and hands against the tall pane that paralleled the front door. As I pulled into the drive, I would see them: Andrea and Jenna, a head taller than her sister, squeezed into the frame. Seeing me, they squealed. My, how they jumped and clapped. You'd think someone had switched their M&M's for coffee beans. No returning Caesar ever felt more welcomed. As I opened the door, they tackled my knees and flooded the entryway with tsunami-size joy.

Their father was home.

It's been too long since I searched for God that way. Too seldom do I hear thunder and think, Is that God? I've been known to let a day, even two, pass without a glance to the eastern sky. Let's do better. "Let heaven fill your thoughts. Do not think only about things down here on earth" (Col. 3:2 NLT).

How about regular ladle dips into the well of God's grace? Drink deeply, my friend. And drink daily.

Max Lucado

GOD'S GIFTS . . .

Have you ever wondered why God gives so much? We could exist on far less. He could have left the world flat and gray; we wouldn't have known the difference. But he didn't.

He splashed orange in the sunrise
and cast the sky in blue.
And if you love to see geese as they gather,
chances are you'll see that too.
Did he have to make the squirrel's tail furry?
Was he obliged to make the birds sing?
And the funny way that chickens scurry
or the majesty of thunder when it rings?
Why give a flower fragrance?
Why give food its taste?
Could it be
he loves to see
that look upon your face?

If we give gifts to show our love, how much more would he? If we—speckled with foibles and greed—love to give gifts, how much more does God, pure and perfect God, enjoy giving gifts to us?

He Chose the Nails

GRACE

FOR THE MOMENT®

January

I have chosen the way of truth.

—Psalm 119:30

Packed for a Purpose

He has filled them with skill.

EXODUS 35:35 NKJV

 You were born prepacked. God looked at your entire life, determined your assignment, and gave you the tools to do the job.

Before traveling, you do something similar. You consider the demands of the journey and pack accordingly. Cold weather? Bring a jacket. Business meeting? Carry the laptop. Time with grandchildren? Better take some sneakers and pain medication.

God did the same with you. *Joe will research animals . . . install curiosity. Meagan will lead a private school . . . an extra dose of management. I need Eric to comfort the sick . . . include a healthy share of compassion. Denalyn will marry Max . . . instill a double portion of patience.*

God packed you on purpose for a purpose.

Cure for the Common Life

The Lord Is With Me

You are with me;
Your rod and Your staff, they comfort me.

PSALM 23:4 NKJV

"You are with me."

Yes, you, Lord, are in heaven. Yes, you rule the universe. Yes, you sit upon the stars and make your home in the deep. But yes, yes, yes, you are with me.

The Lord is with me. The Creator is with me. Yahweh is with me.

Moses proclaimed it: "What great nation has a god as near to them as the Lord our God is near to us" (Deut. 4:7 NLT).

Paul announced it: "He is not far from each one of us" (Acts 17:27 NIV).

And David discovered it: "You are with me."

Somewhere in the pasture, wilderness, or palace, David discovered that God meant business when he said: "I will not leave you" (Gen. 28:15).

Traveling Light

Loaded with Love

He . . . loads me with love and mercy.

PSALM 103:4

It's time to let God's love cover all things in your life. All secrets. All hurts. All hours of evil, minutes of worry.

The mornings you awoke in the bed of a stranger? His love will cover that. The years you peddled prejudice and pride? His love will cover that. Every promise broken, drug taken, penny stolen. Every cross word, cuss word, and harsh word. His love covers all things.

Let it. Discover along with the psalmist: "He . . . loads me with love and mercy." Picture a giant dump truck full of love. There you are behind it. God lifts the bed until the love starts to slide. Slowly at first, then down, down, down until you are hidden, buried, covered in his love.

"Hey, where are you?" someone asks.

"In here, covered in love."

A Love Worth Giving

The Author of Life

He who was dead sat up and began to speak.
And [Jesus] presented him to his mother.

LUKE 7:15 NKJV

The mourners didn't cause him to stop.
Nor did the large crowd, or even the body
of the dead man on the stretcher. It was the
woman—the look on her face and the redness in
her eyes. He knew immediately what was
happening. It was her son who was being carried
out, her only son. And if anyone knows the pain
that comes from losing your only son, God does.

So he did it; he went into action. "Don't cry,"
he told the mother. "Arise!" he told the boy. The
dead man spoke, the devil ran, and the people
were reminded of this truth: For those who know
the Author of Life, death is nothing more than
Satan's dead-man's-bluff.

God Came Near

God Honors Work

Whatever work you do, do your best.

ECCLESIASTES 9:10

Heaven's calendar has seven Sundays a week. God sanctifies each day. He conducts holy business at all hours and in all places. He uncommons the common by turning kitchen sinks into shrines, cafes into convents, and nine-to-five workdays into spiritual adventures.

Workdays? Yes, workdays. He ordained your work as something good. Before he gave Adam a wife or a child, even before he gave Adam britches, God gave Adam a job. "Then the LORD God took the man and put him into the garden of Eden to cultivate it and keep it" (Gen. 2:15 NASB). Innocence, not indolence, characterized the first family. . . .

God unilaterally calls all the physically able to till the gardens he gives. God honors work. So honor God in your work.

Cure for the Common Life

Miraculous Moments

In Christ there is all of God in a human body.

COLOSSIANS 2:9 TLB

Jesus was not a godlike man, nor a manlike God. He was God-man.

Midwifed by a carpenter.

Bathed by a peasant girl.

The maker of the world with a bellybutton.

The author of the Torah being taught the Torah.

Heaven's human. And because he was, we are left with scratch-your-head, double-blink, what's-wrong-with-this-picture? moments like these:

A cripple sponsoring the town dance.

A sack lunch satisfying five thousand tummies.

What do we do with such moments?

What do we do with such a person? We applaud men for doing good things. We enshrine God for doing great things. But when a man does God things?

One thing is certain, we can't ignore him.

Next Door Savior

We Need a Big God

"I am Yahweh."

EXODUS 6:2 JB

The Israelites considered the name *Yahweh* too holy to be spoken by human lips. Whenever they needed to say *Yahweh*, they substituted the word *Adonai*, which means "Lord." If the name needed to be written, the scribes would take a bath before they wrote it and destroy the pen afterward.

The name I AM sounds strikingly close to the Hebrew verb *to be—havah*. It's quite possibly a combination of the present tense form (I am) and the causative tense (I cause to be). *Yahweh*, then, seems to mean "I AM" and "I cause." God is the "One who is" and the "One who causes."

Why is that important? Because we need a big God. And if God is the "One who is," then he is an unchanging God.

Traveling Light

A Yoke of Kindness

Take My yoke upon you and learn from Me,
for I am gentle and lowly in heart,
and you will find rest for your souls.

MATTHEW 11:29 NKJV

Farmers in ancient Israel used to train an inexperienced ox by yoking it to an experienced one with a wooden harness. The straps around the older animal were tightly drawn. He carried the load. But the yoke around the younger animal was loose. He walked alongside the more mature ox, but his burden was light. In this verse Jesus is saying, "I walk alongside you. We are yoked together. But I pull the weight and carry the burden."

I wonder, how many burdens is Jesus carrying for us that we know nothing about? We're aware of some. He carries our sin. He carries our shame. He carries our eternal debt. But are there others? Has he lifted fears before we felt them? Has he carried our confusion so we wouldn't have to? Those times when we have been surprised by our own sense of peace? Could it be that Jesus has lifted our anxiety onto his shoulders and placed a yoke of kindness on ours?

A Love Worth Giving

Our Compassionate Christ

*"Father, forgive them, for they
do not know what they are doing."*

LUKE 23:34 NIV

Have you ever wondered how Jesus kept
from retaliating against the mob that killed
him? Have you ever asked how he kept his
control? Here's the answer. It's . . . this statement:
"for they do not know what they are doing."
Look carefully. It's as if Jesus considered this
bloodthirsty, death-hungry crowd not as
murderers, but as victims. It's as if he saw in their
faces not hatred but confusion. It's as if he
regarded them not as a militant mob but, as he
put it, as "sheep without a shepherd."

"They don't know what they are doing."

And when you think about it, they didn't.
They hadn't the faintest idea what they were
doing. They were a stir-crazy mob, mad at
something they couldn't see so they took it out
on, of all people, God. But they didn't know what
they were doing.

*No Wonder They
Call Him the Savior*

Headed Home

He chose us in Him before the foundation of the world.

EPHESIANS 1:4 NKJV

Search the faces of the Cap Haitian orphanage for Carinette. . . . The girl with the long nose and bushy hair and a handful of photos. . . . The photos bear the images of her future family. She's been adopted.

Her adoptive parents are friends of mine. They brought her pictures, a teddy bear, granola bars, and cookies. Carinette shared the goodies and asked the director to guard her bear, but she keeps the pictures. They remind her of her home-to-be. Within a month, two at the most, she'll be there. She knows the day is coming. . . . Any day now her father will appear. He came once to claim her. He'll come again to carry her home. Till then she lives with a heart headed home.

Shouldn't we all? Our Father paid us a visit too. Have we not been claimed? Adopted? . . . God searched you out. Before you knew you needed adopting, he'd already filed the papers and selected the wallpaper for your room.

Come Thirsty

The Gift of Choice

I haven chosen the way of truth;
I have obeyed your laws.

PSALM 119:30

 We can choose:
a narrow gate or a wide gate (Matt. 7:13–14)
a narrow road or a wide road (Matt. 7:13–14)
the big crowd or the small crowd (Matt. 7:13–14)
We can choose to:
build on rock or sand (Matt. 7:24–27)
serve God or riches (Matt. 6:24)
be numbered among the sheep or the goats (Matt. 25:32–33)

God gives eternal choices, and these choices have eternal consequences.

One of God's greatest gifts? The gift of choice.

He Chose the Nails

Ask and Believe

"If you believe, you will get anything you ask for in prayer."

"If you believe, you will get anything you ask for in prayer."

Don't reduce this grand statement to the category of new cars and paychecks. Don't limit the promise of this passage to the selfish pool of perks and favors. The fruit God assures is far greater than earthly wealth. His dreams are much greater than promotions and proposals.

God wants you to fly. He wants you to fly free of yesterday's guilt. He wants you to fly free of today's fears. He wants you to fly free of tomorrow's grave. Sin, fear, and death. These are the mountains he has moved. These are the prayers he will answer. That is the fruit he will grant. This is what he longs to do.

And the Angels Were Silent

He Lives In You

*I work and struggle, using Christ's great strength
that works so powerfully in me.*

COLOSSIANS 1:29

God was *with* Adam and Eve, walking with
them in the cool of the evening.

God was *with* Abraham, even calling the
patriarch his friend.

God was *with* Moses and the children of
Israel. . . . He was *with* the apostles. Peter could
touch God's beard. John could watch God sleep.
Multitudes could hear his voice. God was *with*
them!

But he is *in* you. . . . He will do what you
cannot. Imagine a million dollars being deposited
into your checking account. To any observer you
look the same, except for the goofy smile, but are
you? Not at all! With God *in* you, you have a
million resources that you did not have before!

Can't stop worrying? Christ can. And he lives
within you.

Can't forgive the jerk, forget the past, or
forsake your bad habits? Christ can! And he lives
within you.

Next Door Savior

Divine Miracles

All things were made by him,
and nothing was made without him.

JOHN 1:3

From where I write I can see several miracles. White-crested waves slap the beach with rhythmic regularity. One after the other the rising swells of salt water gain momentum, humping, rising, then standing to salute the beach before crashing onto the sand. How many billions of times has this simple mystery repeated itself since time began?

In the distance lies a miracle of colors—twins of blue. The ocean-blue of the Atlantic encounters the pale blue of the sky, separated only by the horizon. . . .

Miracles. Divine miracles.

These are miracles because they are mysteries. Scientifically explainable? Yes. Reproducible? To a degree.

But still they are mysteries. Events that stretch beyond our understanding and find their origins in another realm. They are every bit as divine as divided seas, walking cripples, and empty tombs.

God Came Near

Know Your Knack

*Make a careful exploration of who you are and the work
you have been given, and then sink yourself into that.*

GALATIANS 6:4 MSG

God never prefabs or mass-produces people.
No slapdash shaping. "I make all things
new," he declares (Rev. 21:5 NKJV). He didn't hand
you your granddad's bag or your aunt's life; he
personally and deliberately packed *you*. . . .

You can do something no one else can do in a
fashion no one else can do it. Exploring and
extracting your uniqueness excites you, honors
God, and expands his kingdom. So "make a careful
exploration of who you are and the work you have
been given, and then sink yourself into that."

Discover and deploy your knacks. . . .
When you do the most what you do the best,
you put a smile on God's face. What could be
better than that?

Cure for the Common Life

26   MAX LUCADO

Water of Eternal Life

The water I give will become a spring of water gushing
up inside that person, giving eternal life.

JOHN 4:14

Remember the words of Jesus to the Samaritan woman? "The water I give will become a spring of water gushing up inside that person, giving eternal life." Jesus offers, not a singular drink of water, but a perpetual artesian well! And the well isn't a hole in your backyard but the Holy Spirit of God in your heart.

"If anyone believes in me, rivers of living water will flow out from that person's heart, as the Scripture says." Jesus was talking about the Holy Spirit. The Spirit had not yet been given, because Jesus had not yet been raised to glory. But later, those who believed in Jesus would receive the Spirit (John 7:38–39).

Water, in this verse, is a picture of the Spirit of Jesus working in us. He's not working to save us, mind you; that work is done. He's working to change us.

He Chose the Nails

A Worry-Free Life

Do not worry about anything, but pray
and ask God for everything you need.

PHILIPPIANS 4:6

Look around you. You have reason to
worry. The sun blasts cancer-causing rays.
Air vents blow lung-clotting molds. Potato chips
have too many carbs. Vegetables, too many toxins.
And do they have to call an airport a terminal? . . .

Some of us have postgraduate degrees from
the University of Anxiety. We go to sleep worried
that we won't wake up; we wake up worried that
we didn't sleep. We worry that someone will
discover that lettuce was fattening all along. The
mother of one teenager bemoaned, "My daughter
doesn't tell me anything. I'm a nervous wreck."
Another mother replied, "My daughter tells me
everything. I'm a nervous wreck." Wouldn't you
love to stop worrying? Could you use a strong
shelter from life's harsh elements?

God offers you just that: the possibility of a
worry-free life. Not just less worry, but no worry.

Come Thirsty

We Need a Savior

Christ was offered once to bear the sins of many.

HEBREWS 9:28 NKJV

You can't forgive me for my sins nor can I forgive you for yours. Two kids in a mud puddle can't clean each other. They need someone clean. Someone spotless. We need someone clean too.

That's why we need a savior.

Trying to make it to heaven on our own goodness is like trying to get to the moon on a moon beam; nice idea, but try it and see what happens.

Listen. Quit trying to quench your own guilt. You can't do it. There's no way. Not with a bottle of whiskey or perfect Sunday school attendance. Sorry. I don't care how bad you are. You can't be bad enough to forget it. And I don't care how good you are. You can't be good enough to overcome it.

You need a Savior.

No Wonder They Call Him the Savior

The Cure for Selfishness

> *If there is any fellowship of the Spirit,*
> *if any affection and compassion,*
> *make my joy complete by being of the same mind.*

PHILIPPIANS 2:2 NASB

What's the cure for selfishness?

Get your self out of your eye by getting your eye off your self. Quit staring at that little self, and focus on your great Savior.

A friend who is an Episcopalian minister explains the reason he closes his prayers with the sign of the cross. "The touching of my forehead and chest makes a capital 'I.' The gesture of touching first one shoulder, then the other, cuts the 'I' in half."

Isn't that a work of the Cross? A smaller "I" and a greater Christ? Don't focus on yourself; focus on all that you have in Christ. Focus on the fellowship of the Spirit, the affection and compassion of heaven.

A Love Worth Giving

One Step at a Time

*Your word is like a lamp for my feet
and a light for my path.*

PSALM 119:105

Arthur Hays Sulzberger was the publisher of the New York Times during the Second World War. Because of the world conflict, he found it almost impossible to sleep. He was never able to banish worries from his mind until he adopted as his motto these five words—"one step enough for me"—taken from the hymn "Lead Kindly Light."

God isn't going to let you see the distant scene either. So you might as well quit looking for it. He promises a lamp unto our feet, not a crystal ball into the future. We do not need to know what will happen tomorrow.

God is leading you. Leave tomorrow's problems until tomorrow.

Traveling Light

God Never Gives Up

God's business is putting things right.

<small>PSALM 11:7 THE MESSAGE</small>

God never gives up.

When Joseph was dropped into a pit by his own brothers, God didn't give up.

When Moses said, "Here I am, send Aaron," God didn't give up.

When the delivered Israelites wanted Egyptian slavery instead of milk and honey, God didn't give up.

When Peter worshiped him at the supper and cursed him at the fire, he didn't give up.

And when human hands fastened the divine hands to a cross with spikes, it wasn't the soldiers who held the hands of Jesus steady. It was God who held them steady. God, who would give up his only son before he'd give up on you.

Six Hours One Friday

Applaud Loud and Often

Sing to Him, sing psalms to Him;
talk of all His wondrous works!

PSALM 105:2 NKJV

God has never taken his eyes off you. Not for a millisecond. He's always near. He lives to hear your heartbeat. He loves to hear your prayers. He'd die for your sin before he'd let you die in your sin, so he did.

What do you do with such a Savior? Don't you sing to him? Don't you declare, confess, and proclaim his name? Don't you bow a knee, lower a head, hammer a nail, feed the poor, and lift up your gift in worship? Of course you do.

Worship God. Applaud him loud and often. For your sake, you need it.

And for heaven's sake, he deserves it.

Cure for the Common Life

Love Accepts All Things

> *Love . . . bears all things, believes*
> *all things, hopes all things, endures all things.*
>
> 1 Corinthians 13:4–7 nkjv

Wouldn't it be nice if love were like a cafeteria line? What if you could look at the person with whom you live and select what you want and pass on what you don't? What if parents could do this with kids? "I'll take a plate of good grades and cute smiles, and I'm passing on the teenage identity crisis and tuition bills."

What if kids could do the same with parents? "Please give me a helping of allowances and free lodging but no rules or curfews, thank you."

And spouse with spouse? "H'm, how about a bowl of good health and good moods. But job transfers, in-laws, and laundry are not on my diet."

Wouldn't it be great if love were like a cafeteria line? It would be easier. It would be neater. It would be painless and peaceful. But you know what? It wouldn't be love. Love doesn't accept just a few things. Love is willing to accept all things.

A Love Worth Giving

Our Work Is God's Work

Jesus got into one of the boats, . . . that belonged to [Peter], and asked him to push off a little from the land.

LUKE 5:3

Jesus claims Peter's boat. He doesn't *request* the use of it. Christ doesn't fill out an application or ask permission; he simply boards the boat and begins to preach.

He can do that, you know. All boats belong to Christ. Your boat is where you spend your day, make your living, and to a large degree live your life. The taxi you drive, . . . the dental office you manage, the family you feed and transport—this is your boat. Christ shoulder-taps us and reminds:

"You drive my truck."

"You work on my job site."

"You serve my hospital wing."

To us all, Jesus says, "Your work is my work."

Cure for the Common Life

Love for the Least

*"I was hungry, and you gave me food. I was thirsty,
and you gave me something to drink."*

MATTHEW 25:35

What is the sign of the saved? Their
scholarship? Their willingness to go to
foreign lands? Their ability to amass an audience
and preach? Their skillful pens and hope-filled
volumes? Their great miracles? No.

The sign of the saved is their love for the least.

Those put on the right hand of God will be
those who gave food to the hungry, drink to
the thirsty, warmth to the lonely, clothing to the
naked, comfort to the sick, and friendship to
the imprisoned.

Did you note how simple the works are? Jesus
doesn't say, "I was sick and you healed me. . . .
I was in prison and you liberated me. . . . I was
lonely and you built a retirement home for me. . . ."
He doesn't say, "I was thirsty and you gave me
spiritual counsel."

No fanfare. No hoopla. No media coverage.
Just good people doing good things.

And the Angels Were Silent

Blind Ambition

*Before destruction the heart of a man is haughty,
and before honor is humility.*

PROVERBS 18:12 NKJV

Blind ambition. Success at all cost.
Becoming a legend in one's own time.
Climbing the ladder to the top. King of the
mountain. Top of the heap. "I did it my way."

We make heroes out of people who are
ambitious. We hold them up as models for our
kids and put their pictures on the covers of
our magazines.

And rightly so. This world would be in sad
shape without people who dream of touching the
heavens. Ambition is that grit in the soul which
creates disenchantment with the ordinary and
puts the dare into dreams.

But left unchecked it becomes an insatiable
addiction to power and prestige; a roaring hunger
for achievement that devours people as a lion
devours an animal, leaving behind only the
skeletal remains of relationships. . . .

God won't tolerate it. . . . Blind ambition is a
giant step away from God and one step closer to
catastrophe.

God Came Near

Look at the Son

Let us run with endurance the race that is set before us,
looking unto Jesus, the author and finisher of our faith.

HEBREWS 12:1–2 NKJV

More mornings than not I drag myself out
of bed and onto the street. . . . I run because
I don't like cardiologists.

Since heart disease runs in our family, I run
in our neighborhood. As the sun is rising, I am
running. And as I am running, my body is
groaning. It doesn't want to cooperate. My knee
hurts. My hip is stiff. My ankles complain. . . .

Things hurt. And as things hurt, I've learned
that I have three options. Go home. (Denalyn
would laugh at me.) Meditate on my hurts until I
start imagining I'm having chest pains. (Pleasant
thought.) Or I can keep running and watch the
sun come up. . . . If I watch God's world go from
dark to golden, guess what? The same happens to
my attitude. The pain passes and the joints
loosen. . . . Everything improves as I fix my eyes
on the sun.

Wasn't that the counsel of the Hebrew
epistle—"looking unto Jesus"?

Traveling Light

Two Sisters

*Since we have been made right with God
by our faith, we have peace with God.*

ROMANS 5:1

Pride and shame. You'd never know they are sisters. They appear so different. Pride puffs out her chest. Shame hangs her head. Pride boasts. Shame hides. Pride seeks to be seen. Shame seeks to be avoided.

But don't be fooled, the emotions have the same parentage. And the emotions have the same impact. They keep you from your Father.

Pride says, "You're too good for him."

Shame says, "You're too bad for him."

Pride drives you away.

Shame keeps you away.

If pride is what goes before a fall, then shame is what keeps you from getting up after one.

He Chose the Nails

An Everlasting Love

As high as the sky is above the earth,
so great is his love for those who respect him.

PSALM 103:11

The big news of the Bible is not that you love God but that God loves you; not that you can know God but that God already knows you! He tattooed your name on the palm of his hand. His thoughts of you outnumber the sand on the shore. You never leave his mind, escape his sight, flee his thoughts. He sees the worst of you and loves you still. Your sins of tomorrow and failings of the future will not surprise him; he sees them now. Every day and deed of your life has passed before his eyes and been calculated in his decision. He knows you better than you know you and has reached his verdict: he loves you still. No discovery will disillusion him; no rebellion will dissuade him. He loves you with an everlasting love.

Come Thirsty

The World Needs Servants

The Son of Man did not come to be served,
but to serve, and to give His life a ransom for many.

MARK 10:45 NKJV

The world needs servants. People like Jesus who "did not come to be served, but to serve." He chose remote Nazareth over center-stage Jerusalem, his dad's carpentry shop over a marble-columned palace, and three decades of anonymity over a life of popularity.

Jesus came to serve. He selected prayer over sleep, the wilderness over the Jordan, irascible apostles over obedient angels. I'd have gone with the angels. Given the choice, I would have built my apostle team out of cherubim and seraphim or Gabriel and Michael, eyewitnesses of Red Sea rescues and Mount Carmel falling fires. I'd choose the angels.

Not Jesus. He picked the people. Peter, Andrew, John, and Matthew. When they feared the storm, he stilled it. When they had no coin for taxes, he supplied it. And when they had no wine for the wedding or food for the multitude, he made both.

Cure for the Common Life

The Last Step

He will change our simple bodies
and make them like his own glorious body.

PHILIPPIANS 3:21

 Which word describes your body? My *cancerous* body? My *arthritic* body? My *deformed* body? My *crippled* body? My *addicted* body? My *ever-expanding* body? The word may be different, but the message is the same: These bodies are weak. They began decaying the minute we began breathing.

And, according to God, that's a part of the plan. Every wrinkle and every needle take us one step closer to the last step when Jesus will change our simple bodies into forever bodies. No pain. No depression. No sickness. No end.

This is not our forever house. It will serve for the time being. But there is nothing like the moment we enter his door.

Traveling Light

February

I will extol You, O Lord, for You have lifted me up.

—Psalm 30:1 NKJV

Have You Seen Him?

"We were eyewitnesses of His majesty."

2 PETER 1:16 NKJV

Jesus. The man. The bronzed Galilean who spoke with such thunderous authority and loved with such childlike humility.

The one who claimed to be older than time and greater than death. . . .

Have you seen him?

Those who first did were never the same.

"My Lord and my God!" cried Thomas.

"I have seen the Lord," exclaimed Mary Magdalene.

"We have seen his glory," declared John.

"Were not our hearts burning within us while he talked?" rejoiced the two Emmaus-bound disciples.

But Peter said it best. "We were eyewitnesses of his majesty."

God Came Near

Living Loved

*God showed how much he loved us by sending his only
Son into the world. . . . This is real love.*

1 JOHN 4:9 NLT

Apart from God, "the heart is deceitful
above all things" (Jer. 17:9 NIV). A marriage-
saving love is not within us. A friendship-preserving
devotion cannot be found in our hearts. We need
help from an outside source. A transfusion.
Would we love as God loves? Then we start by
receiving God's love.

We preachers have been guilty of skipping
the first step. "Love each other!" we tell our
churches. "Be patient, kind, forgiving," we urge.
But instructing people to love without telling
them they are loved is like telling them to write a
check without our making a deposit in their
accounts. No wonder so many relationships are
overdrawn. Hearts have insufficient love.

The secret to loving is living loved.

A Love Worth Giving

Defined by Grace

Christ . . . raised us up together . . . that . . .
He might show the exceeding riches of His grace.

EPHESIANS 2:5–6 NKJV

Grace defines you. As grace sinks in, earthly labels fade. Society labels you like a can on an assembly line. Stupid. Unproductive. Slow learner. Fast talker. Quitter. Cheapskate. But as grace infiltrates, criticism disintegrates. You know you aren't who they say you are. You are who God says you are. Spiritually alive. Heavenly positioned. Connected to the Father. A billboard of mercy. An honored child.

Of course, not all labels are negative. Some people regard you as handsome, clever, successful, or efficient. But even a White House office doesn't compare with being "seated with him in the heavenly realms" (Eph. 2:6 NLT). Grace creates the Christian's résumé.

Come Thirsty

A Quiet Day of Rest

Remember to keep the Sabbath holy.

EXODUS 20:8

Ever feel the wheels of your life racing faster and faster as you speed past the people you love? Could you use a reminder on how to slow it all down?

If so, read what Jesus did during the last Sabbath of his life. Start in the Gospel of Matthew. Didn't find anything? Try Mark. Read what Mark recorded about the way Jesus spent the Sabbath. Nothing there either? Strange. What about Luke? What does Luke say? Not a reference to the day? Not a word about it? Well, try John. Surely John mentions the Sabbath. He doesn't? No reference? Hmmmm. Looks like Jesus was quiet that day.

"Wait a minute. That's it?" That's it.

"You mean with one week left to live, Jesus observed the Sabbath?" As far as we can tell.

"You mean with all those apostles to train and people to teach, he took a day to rest and worship?" Apparently so.

And the Angels Were Silent

Love Isn't Easy

Love your enemies. Pray for those who hurt you.

Love isn't easy. Not for you. Not for me. Not even for Jesus. Want proof? Listen to his frustration: "You people have no faith. How long must I stay with you? How long must I put up with you?" (Mark 9:19).

How long must I put up with you?

"Long enough to be called crazy by my brothers and a liar by my neighbors. Long enough to be run out of my town and my Temple. . . ."

How long? "Until the rooster sings and the sweat stings and the mallet rings and a hillside of demons smirk at a dying God."

How long? "Long enough for every sin to so soak my sinless soul that heaven will turn in horror until my swollen lips pronounce the final transaction: 'It is finished.'"

How long? "Until it kills me."

A Love Worth Giving

A Next Door Savior

"Who is this? Even the wind and the waves obey him!"

MARK 4:41

He was, at once, man and God.

There he was, the single most significant person who ever lived. Forget MVP; he is the entire league. The head of the parade? Hardly. No one else shares the street. Who comes close? Humanity's best and brightest fade like dime-store rubies next to him.

Dismiss him? We can't.

Resist him? Equally difficult. Don't we need a God-man Savior? A just-God Jesus could make us but not understand us. A just-man Jesus could love us but never save us. But a God-man Jesus? Near enough to touch. Strong enough to trust. A next door Savior.

A Savior found by millions to be irresistible.

Next Door Savior

Our Unchanging God

"When you go to the people of Israel, tell them, 'I AM *sent me to you.'"*

Do you know anyone who goes around saying, "I am"? Neither do I. When we say "I am," we always add another word. "I am *happy.*" "I am *sad.*" "I am *strong.*" "I am *Max.*" God, however, starkly states, "I AM" and adds nothing else.

"You are what?" we want to ask. "I AM," he replies. God needs no descriptive word because he never changes. God is what he is. He is what he has always been. His immutability motivated the psalmist to declare, "But thou art the same" (Ps. 102:27 KJV). The writer is saying, "You are the One who is. You never change." Yahweh is an unchanging God.

Traveling Light

Kindness Makes the Coffee

He is kind even to people who are ungrateful and full of sin.

How often do we thank God for his kindness? Not often enough. But does our ingratitude restrict his kindness? No. "Because he is kind even to people who are ungrateful and full of sin."

In the original language, the word for *kindness* carries an added idea the English word does not. Chiefly it refers to an act of grace. But it also refers to a deed or person who is "useful, serviceable, adapted to its purpose." *Kindness* was even employed to describe food that was tasty as well as healthy. Sounds odd to our ears. "Hey, honey, what a great meal. The salad is especially *kind* tonight."

But the usage makes sense. Isn't kindness good *and* good for you? Pleasant *and* practical? Kindness not only says "good morning," kindness makes the coffee.

A Love Worth Giving

An Amazing Destiny

I will extol You, O LORD, for You have lifted me up.

PSALM 30:1 NKJV

In God's book man is heading somewhere. He has an amazing destiny. We are being prepared to walk down the church aisle and become the bride of Jesus. We are going to live with him. Share the throne with him. Reign with him. We count. We are valuable. And what's more, our worth is built in! Our value is inborn.

You see, if there was anything that Jesus wanted everyone to understand it was this: A person is worth something simply because he is a person. That is why he treated people like he did. Think about it. The girl caught making undercover thunder with someone she shouldn't—he forgave her. The untouchable leper who asked for cleansing—he touched him. And the blind welfare case that cluttered the roadside—he honored him. And the worn-out old windbag addicted to self-pity near the pool of Siloam—he healed him!

No Wonder They Call Him the Savior

The Place of Prayer

They went back to Jerusalem from the Mount of Olives. . . . They all continued praying together.

ACTS 1:12, 14

Desire power for your life? . . . It will come as you pray. For ten days the disciples prayed. Ten days of prayer plus a few minutes of preaching led to three thousand saved souls. Perhaps we invert the numbers. We're prone to pray for a few minutes and preach for ten days. Not the apostles. Like the boat waiting for Christ, they lingered in his presence. They never left the place of prayer. . . .

The Upper Room was occupied by 120 disciples. Since there were about 4,000,000 people in Palestine at the time, this means that fewer than 1 in 30,000 was a Christian. Yet look at the fruit of their work. Better said, look at the fruit of God's Spirit in them. We can only wonder what would happen today if we, who *still* struggle, did what they did: wait on the Lord in the right place.

Come Thirsty

Freedom to Choose

We are people who have faith and are saved.

HEBREWS 10:39

God honors us with the freedom to choose where we spend eternity.

And what an honor it is! In so many areas of life we have no choice. Think about it. You didn't choose your gender. You didn't choose your siblings. You didn't choose your race or place of birth.

Sometimes our lack of choices angers us. "It's not fair," we say. It's not fair that I was born in poverty or that I sing so poorly or that I run so slowly. But the scales of life were forever tipped on the side of fairness when God planted a tree in the Garden of Eden. All complaints were silenced when Adam and his descendants were given free will, the freedom to make whatever eternal choice we desire. Any injustice in this life is offset by the honor of choosing our destiny in the next.

He Chose the Nails

No Price Is Too High

"We had to celebrate and be happy because your brother . . . was lost, but now he is found."

LUKE 15:32

When our oldest daughter, Jenna, was two, I lost her in a department store. One minute she was at my side and the next she was gone. I panicked. All of a sudden only one thing mattered—I had to find my daughter. Shopping was forgotten. The list of things I came to get was unimportant. I yelled her name. What people thought didn't matter. For a few minutes, every ounce of energy had one goal—to find my lost child. (I did, by the way. She was hiding behind some jackets!)

No price is too high for a parent to pay to redeem his child. No energy is too great. No effort too demanding. A parent will go to any length to find his or her own.

So will God.

Mark it down. God's greatest creation is not the flung stars or the gorged canyons; it's his eternal plan to reach his children.

And the Angels Were Silent

He Chose the Cross

You did not save yourselves; it was a gift from God.

EPHESIANS 2:8

Jesus' obedience began in a small town carpentry shop. His uncommon approach to his common life groomed him for his uncommon call. "When Jesus entered public life he was about thirty years old" (Luke 3:23 MSG). . . . In order for Jesus to change the world, he had to say good-bye to his world.

He had to give Mary a kiss. Have a final meal in the kitchen, a final walk through the streets. Did he ascend one of the hills of Nazareth and think of the day he would ascend the hill near Jerusalem?

He knew what was going to happen. "God chose him for this purpose long before the world began" (1 Pet. 1:20 NLT). Every ounce of suffering had been scripted—it just fell to him to play the part.

Not that he had to. Nazareth was a cozy town. Why not build a carpentry business? Keep his identity a secret? . . . To be forced to die is one thing, but to willingly take up your own cross is something else.

Next Door Savior

"God Is! God Is!"

If I go up to the heavens, you are there;
if I make my bed in the depths, you are there.

PSALM 139:8 NIV

It is the normality not the uniqueness of God's miracles that causes them to be so staggering. Rather than shocking the globe with an occasional demonstration of deity, God has opted to display his power daily. Proverbially. Pounding waves. Prism-cast colors. Birth, death, life. We are surrounded by miracles. God is throwing testimonies at us like fireworks, each one exploding, "God is! God is!"

The psalmist marveled at such holy handiwork. "Where can I go from your Spirit?" he questioned with delight. "Where can I flee from your presence? If I go up to the heavens, you are there; if I make my bed in the depths, you are there" (Ps. 139:7–8 NIV).

We wonder, with so many miraculous testimonies around us, how we could escape God. But somehow we do. We live in an art gallery of divine creativity and yet are content to gaze only at the carpet.

God Came Near

You Are God's Idea

"Before I made you in your mother's womb, I chose you."

JEREMIAH 1:5

God planned and packed you on purpose for his purpose.

Heaven's custom design.

At a moment before moments existed, the sovereign Star Maker resolved, "I will make _____." Your name goes in the blank. Then he continued with, "And I will make him/her _____, _____ and _____ and _____ and _____." Fill those blanks with your characteristics. Insightful. Clever. Detail oriented. Restless. And since you are God's idea, you are a good idea. What God said about Jeremiah, he said about you: "Before I made you in your mother's womb, I chose you. Before you were born, I set you apart for a special work."

Set apart for a special work.

Cure for the Common Life

A Daily Development

*God is working in you to help you
want to do and be able to do what pleases him.*

PHILIPPIANS 2:13

Wouldn't a bride and groom have to be more married on their fiftieth anniversary than on their wedding day?

Yet, on the other hand, how could they be? The marriage certificate hasn't matured. Ah, but the relationship has, and there is the difference. Technically, they are no more united than they were when they left the altar. But relationally, they are completely different.

The same is true of our walk with God. Can you be more saved than you were the first day of your salvation? No. But can a person grow in salvation? Absolutely. It, like marriage, is a done deal and a daily development.

He Chose the Nails

Why Worry?

Continue praying, keeping alert,
and always thanking God.

COLOSSIANS 4:2

Two words summarize Christ's opinion of worry: *irrelevant* and *irreverent.*

"Can all your worries add a single moment to your life? Of course not" (Matt. 6:27 NLT). Worry is irrelevant. It alters nothing. When was the last time you solved a problem by worrying about it? Imagine someone saying, "I got behind in my bills, so I resolved to worry my way out of debt. And, you know, it worked! A few sleepless nights, a day of puking and hand wringing. I yelled at my kids and took some pills, and—glory to worry— money appeared on my desk."

It doesn't happen! Worry changes nothing. You don't add one day to your life or one bit of life to your day by worrying. Your anxiety earns you heartburn, nothing more. . . .

Ninety-two percent of our worries are needless! Not only is worry irrelevant, doing nothing; worry is irreverent, distrusting God.

Come Thirsty

The Reason for the Cross

We have been sanctified through the offering of the body of Jesus Christ once for all.

HEBREWS 10:10 NKJV

Man by himself cannot deal with his own guilt. He must have help from the outside. In order to forgive himself, he must have forgiveness from the one he has offended. Yet man is unworthy to ask God for forgiveness.

That, then, is the whole reason for the cross.

The cross did what sacrificed lambs could not do. It erased our sins, not for a year, but for eternity. The cross did what man could not do. It granted us the right to talk with, love, and even live with God.

You can't do that by yourself. I don't care how many worship services you attend or good deeds you do, your goodness is insufficient. You can't be good enough to deserve forgiveness. No one bats a thousand. No one bowls three hundred. No one. Not you, not me, not anyone.

That's why we need a savior.

No Wonder They Call Him the Savior

Reasons for Joy

Rejoice in the Lord always. Again I will say, rejoice!

PHILIPPIANS 4:4 NKJV

"How's life?" someone asks. And we who've been resurrected from the dead say, "Well, things could be better." Or "Couldn't get a parking place." Or "My parents won't let me move to Hawaii." Or "People won't leave me alone so I can finish my sermon on selfishness." . . .

Are you so focused on what you don't have that you are blind to what you do?

You have a ticket to heaven no thief can take,
an eternal home no divorce can break.

Every sin of your life has been cast to the sea.
Every mistake you've made is nailed to the tree.

You're blood-bought and heaven-made.
A child of God—forever saved.

So be grateful, joyful—for isn't it true?
What you don't have is much less
than what you do.

A Love Worth Giving

It's a Jungle Out There!

*My help comes from the LORD, who made
heaven and earth.*

PSALM 121:2

For many people, life is—well, life is a
jungle. Not a jungle of trees and beasts. . . .
Our jungles are comprised of the thicker thickets
of failing health, broken hearts, and empty
wallets. . . . We don't hear the screeching of birds
or the roaring of lions, but we do hear the
complaints of neighbors and the demands
of bosses. . . .

Whether you are a lamb lost on a craggy
ledge or a city slicker alone in a deep jungle,
everything changes when your rescuer appears.

Your loneliness diminishes, because you have
fellowship. Your despair decreases, because you
have vision. Your confusion begins to lift, because
you have direction.

You haven't left the jungle. The trees still
eclipse the sky, and the thorns still cut the skin. . . .
It hasn't changed, but you have. You have changed
because you have hope. And you have hope because
you have met someone who can lead you out.

Traveling Light

Don't Forget

*May our Lord Jesus Christ himself . . . encourage you
and strengthen you in every good thing you do and say.*

2 THESSALONIANS 2:16

Are you still in love with Jesus? Before
you remember anything, remember him.
If you forget anything, don't forget him.

Oh, but how quickly we forget. So much
happens through the years. So many changes
within. So many alterations without. And,
somewhere, back there, we leave him. We don't
turn away from him . . . we just don't take him
with us. Assignments come. Promotions come.
Budgets are made. Kids are born, and the
Christ . . . the Christ is forgotten.

Has it been a while since you stared at the
heavens in speechless amazement? Has it been
a while since you realized God's divinity and
your carnality?

If it has, then you need to know something.
He is still there. He hasn't left.

Six Hours One Friday

God Warrants Our Worship

Oh, give thanks to the LORD, for He is good!
For His mercy endures forever.

PSALM 107:1 NKJV

The chief reason for applauding God? He deserves it. If singing did nothing but weary your voice, if giving only emptied your wallet—if worship did nothing for you—it would still be right to do. God warrants our worship.

How else do you respond to a Being of blazing, blistering, unadulterated, unending holiness? What do you do with such holiness if not adore it?

And his power. He churns forces that launch meteors, orbit planets, and ignite stars. Commanding whales to spout salty air, petunias to perfume the night, and songbirds to chirp joy into spring. Above the earth, flotillas of clouds endlessly shape and reshape; within the earth, strata of groaning rocks shift and turn. Who are we to sojourn on a trembling, wonderful orb so shot through with wonder?

Cure for the Common Life

Working Well

> *"My Father never stops working,*
> *and so I keep working, too."*
>
> JOHN 5:17

God views work worthy of its own engraved commandment: "You shall work six days, but on the seventh day you shall rest" (Exod. 34:21 NASB). We like the second half of that verse. But emphasis on the day of rest might cause us to miss the command to work: "You shall work six days." Whether you work at home or in the marketplace, your work matters to God.

And your work matters to society. We need you! Cities need plumbers. Nations need soldiers. Stoplights break. Bones break. We need people to repair the first and set the second. Someone has to raise kids, raise cane, and manage the kids who raise Cain.

Whether you log on or lace up for the day, you imitate God. Jehovah himself worked for the first six days of creation. Jesus said, "My Father never stops working, and so I keep working, too."

Cure for the Common Life

Assurance of Victory

This is the victory that conquers the world—our faith.

1 JOHN 5:4

 What is unique about the kingdom of God is that you are assured of victory. You have won! You are assured that you will someday stand before the face of God and see the King of kings. You are assured that someday you will enter a world where there will be no more pain, no more tears, no more sorrow.

If you have no faith in the future, then you have no power in the present. If you have no faith in the life beyond this life, then your present life is going to be powerless. But if you believe in the future and are assured of victory, then there should be a dance in your step and a smile on your face.

The Inspirational Study Bible

To See God

> *"Anything you did for even the least*
> *of my people here, you also did for me."*
>
> MATTHEW 25:40

When Francis of Asissi turned his back on wealth to seek God in simplicity, he stripped naked and walked out of the city. He soon encountered a leper on the side of the road. He passed him, then stopped and went back and embraced the diseased man. Francis then continued on his journey. After a few steps he turned to look again at the leper, but no one was there.

For the rest of his life, he believed the leper was Jesus Christ. He may have been right.

Jesus lives in the forgotten. He has taken up residence in the ignored. He has made a mansion amid the ill. If we want to see God, we must go among the broken and beaten and there we will see him.

And the Angels Were Silent

Wisdom in Warnings

Do not be deceived: God cannot be mocked.
A man reaps what he sows.

GALATIANS 6:7 NIV

We're often surprised at life's mishaps, but when pressed against the wall of honesty we have to admit that if we had just fired that silly receptionist and done something about those calls, we could have avoided many problems. We usually knew that trouble was just around the bend. Christians who have fallen away felt the fire waning long before it went out. Unwanted pregnancies or explosions of anger may appear to be the fruit of a moment's waywardness, but in reality, they're usually the result of a history of ignoring warnings about an impending fire.

Are you close to the falls? Are your senses numb? Are your eyes trained to turn and roll when they should pause and observe?

Then maybe you need to repair your warning detector.

God Came Near

Open Your Heart

When I am afraid, I put my trust in you.

PSALM 56:3 NLT

How did Jesus endure the terror of the crucifixion? He went first to the Father with his fears. He modeled the words of Psalm 56:3: "When I am afraid, I put my trust in you."

Do the same with yours. Don't avoid life's Gardens of Gethsemane. Enter them. Just don't enter them alone. And while there, be honest. Pounding the ground is permitted. Tears are allowed. And if you sweat blood, you won't be the first. Do what Jesus did; open your heart.

And be specific. Jesus was. "Take this cup," he prayed. Give God the number of the flight. Tell him the length of the speech. Share the details of the job transfer. He has plenty of time. He also has plenty of compassion.

He doesn't think your fears are foolish or silly. He won't tell you to "buck up" or "get tough." He's been where you are. He knows how you feel.

And he knows what you need.

Traveling Light

The Love of God

I'll call the unloved and make them beloved.

Our love depends on the receiver of the love. Let a thousand people pass before us, and we will not feel the same about each. Our love will be regulated by their appearance, by their personalities. Even when we find a few people we like, our feelings will fluctuate. How they treat us will affect how we love them. The receiver regulates our love.

Not so with the love of God. We have no thermostatic impact on his love for us. The love of God is born from within him, not from what he finds in us. His love is uncaused and spontaneous. . . .

Does he love us because of our goodness? Because of our kindness? Because of our great faith? No, he loves us because of *his* goodness, kindness, and great faith.

A Love Worth Giving

March

"*I am the Holy One,
and I am among you.*"

—Hosea 11:9

The Reward of Christianity

All things are worth nothing compared with the greatness of knowing Christ Jesus my Lord.

PHILIPPIANS 3:8

The reward of Christianity is Christ.

Do you journey to the Grand Canyon for the souvenir T-shirt or the snow globe with the snowflakes that fall when you shake it? No. The reward of the Grand Canyon is the Grand Canyon. The wide-eyed realization that you are part of something ancient, splendid, powerful, and greater than you.

The cache of Christianity is Christ. Not money in the bank or a car in the garage or a healthy body or a better self-image. Secondary and tertiary fruits perhaps. But the Fort Knox of faith is Christ. Fellowship with him. Walking with him. Pondering him. Exploring him. The heart-stopping realization that in him you are part of something ancient, endless, unstoppable, and unfathomable. And that he, who can dig the Grand Canyon with his pinkie, thinks you're worth his death on Roman timber. Christ is the reward of Christianity.

Next Door Savior

Anger Does No Good

An angry person causes trouble.

PROVERBS 29:22

Anger. It's a peculiar yet predictable emotion. It begins as a drop of water. An irritant. A frustration. Nothing big, just an aggravation. Someone gets your parking place. Someone pulls in front of you on the freeway. A waitress is slow and you are in a hurry. The toast burns. Drops of water. Drip. Drip. Drip. Drip.

Yet, get enough of these seemingly innocent drops of anger and before long you've got a bucket full of rage. Walking revenge. Blind bitterness. . . .

Now, is that any way to live? What good has hatred ever brought? What hope has anger ever created? What problems have ever been resolved by revenge?

No Wonder They Call Him the Savior

Our Problem

The wages of sin is death, but the gift of God is eternal life in Christ Jesus our Lord.

ROMANS 6:23

We have a problem: We are not holy, and "anyone whose life is not holy will never see the Lord" (Heb. 12:14).

Our deeds are ugly. Our actions are harsh. We don't do what we want to do, we don't like what we do, and what's worse—yes, there is something worse—we can't change.

We try, oh, how we try. But "Can a leopard change his spots? In the same way, Jerusalem, you cannot change and do good, because you are accustomed to doing evil" (Jer. 13:23).

We, like Adam, were under a curse, but Jesus "changed places with us and put himself under that curse" (Gal. 3:13).

The sinless One took on the face of a sinner so that we sinners could take on the face of a saint.

He Chose the Nails

Work and Worship

Work and get everything done during six days each week,
but the seventh day is a day of rest to honor the LORD.

EXODUS 20:9–10

We need one day in which work comes to a screeching halt. We need one twenty-four-hour period in which the wheels stop grinding and the motor stops turning. We need to stop. . . .

There is a verse that summarizes many lives: "Man is a mere phantom as he goes to and fro: He bustles about, but only in vain; he heaps up wealth, not knowing who will get it" (Ps. 39:6 NIV).

Does that sound like your life? Are you so seldom in one place that your friends regard you as a phantom? Are you so constantly on the move that your family is beginning to question your existence? Do you take pride in your frenzy at the expense of your faith?

Slow down. If God commanded it, you need it. If Jesus modeled it, you need it. . . . Take a day to say no to work and yes to worship.

And the Angels Were Silent

Uncommonly Unique

*I will praise You, for I am fearfully
and wonderfully made.*

PSALM 139:14 NKJV

How would you answer this multiple-
choice question?

I am

_____ a coincidental collision of particles.

_____ an accidental evolution of molecules.

_____ soulless flotsam in the universe.

_____ "fearfully and wonderfully made."

Don't dull your life by missing this point:
You are more than statistical chance, more than a
marriage of heredity and society, more than a
confluence of inherited chromosomes and
childhood trauma. More than a walking weather
vane whipped about by the cold winds of fate.
Thanks to God you have been "sculpted from
nothing into something" (Ps. 139:15 MSG).

Cure for the Common Life

He's Been There

He had to enter into every detail of human life.

HEBREWS 2:17 MSG

You've barely dipped a toe into Matthew's gospel when you realize Jesus hails from the Tilted-Halo Society. Rahab was a Jericho harlot. Grandpa Jacob was slippery enough to warrant an electric ankle bracelet. David had a personality as irregular as a Picasso painting—one day writing psalms, another day seducing his captain's wife. But did Jesus erase his name from the list? Not at all. . . .

Why did Jesus hang his family's dirty laundry on the neighborhood clothesline?

Because your family has some too. The dad who never came home. The grandparent who ran away with the coworker. If your family tree has bruised fruit, then Jesus wants you to know, "I've been there."

The phrase "I've been there" is in the chorus of Christ's theme song. To the lonely, Jesus whispers, "I've been there." To the discouraged, Christ nods his head and sighs, "I've been there."

Next Door Savior

God Has No Limitations

"Where can I go to get away from your Spirit?"

PSALM 139:7

 You and I are governed. The weather determines what we wear. The terrain tells us how to travel. Gravity dictates our speed, and health determines our strength. We may challenge these forces and alter them slightly, but we never remove them.

God—our Shepherd—doesn't check the weather; he makes it. He doesn't defy gravity; he created it. He isn't affected by health; he has no body. Jesus said, "God is spirit" (John 4:24). Since he has no body, he has no limitations—equally active in Cambodia as he is in Connecticut. "Where can I go to get away from your Spirit?" asked David. "Where can I run from you? If I go up to the heavens, you are there. If I lie down in the grave, you are there" (Ps. 139:7–8).

Traveling Light

Kind Hearts

Love suffers long and is kind.

1 Corinthians 13:4 NKJV

What is your kindness quotient? When was the last time you did something kind for someone in your family—e.g., got a blanket, cleaned off the table, prepared the coffee—without being asked?

Think about your school or workplace. Which person is the most overlooked or avoided? A shy student? A grumpy employee? Maybe he doesn't speak the language. Maybe she doesn't fit in. Are you kind to this person?

Kind hearts are quietly kind. They let the car cut into traffic and the young mom with three kids move up in the checkout line. They pick up the neighbor's trash can that rolled into the street. And they are especially kind at church. They understand that perhaps the neediest person they'll meet all week is the one standing in the foyer or sitting on the row behind them in worship. Paul writes: "When we have the opportunity to help anyone, we should do it. But we should give special attention to those who are in the family of believers" (Gal. 6:10).

A Love Worth Giving

The Pioneer of Salvation

He was wounded for our transgressions,
He was bruised for our iniquities.

ISAIAH 53:5 NKJV

The one to whom we pray knows our feelings. He knows temptation. He has felt discouraged. He has been hungry and sleepy and tired. He knows what we feel like when the alarm clock goes off. He knows what we feel like when our children want different things at the same time. He nods in understanding when we pray in anger. He is touched when we tell him there is more to do than can ever be done. He smiles when we confess our weariness.

He wants us to remember that he, too, was human. He wants us to know that he, too, knew the drone of the humdrum and the weariness that comes with long days. He wants us to remember that our trailblazer didn't wear bulletproof vests or rubber gloves or an impenetrable suit of armor. No, he pioneered our salvation through the world that you and I face daily.

No Wonder They Call Him the Savior

Redefining Prayer

Continue earnestly in prayer,
being vigilant in it with thanksgiving.

COLOSSIANS 4:2 NKJV

Early Christians were urged to

- "pray without ceasing" (1 Thess. 5:17 NASB);
- "always be prayerful" (Rom. 12:12 NLT);
- "pray at all times and on every occasion" (Eph. 6:18 NLT).

Sound burdensome? Are you wondering, My business needs attention, my children need dinner, my bills need paying. How can I stay in a place of prayer?

Do this. Change your definition of prayer. Think of prayers less as an activity for God and more as an awareness of God. Seek to live in uninterrupted awareness. Acknowledge his presence everywhere you go. As you stand in line to register your car, think, *Thank you, Lord, for being here.* In the grocery as you shop, *Your presence, my King, I welcome.* As you wash the dishes, worship your Maker.

Come Thirsty

The Sin of the World

Christ carried our sins in his body on the cross. . . .

1 PETER 2:24

Every aspect of the crucifixion was intended not only to hurt the victim but to shame him. Death on a cross was usually reserved for the most vile offenders: slaves, murderers, assassins, and the like. The condemned person was marched through the city streets, shouldering his crossbar and wearing a placard about his neck that named his crime. At the execution site he was stripped and mocked.

Crucifixion was so abhorrent that Cicero wrote, "Let the very name of the cross be far away, not only from the body of a Roman citizen, but even from his thoughts, his eyes, his ears."

Jesus was not only shamed before people, he was shamed before heaven.

Since he bore the sin of the murderer and adulterer, he felt the shame of the murderer and adulterer. Though he never lied, he bore the disgrace of a liar. Though he never cheated, he felt the embarrassment of a cheater. Since he bore the sin of the world, he felt the collective shame of the world.

He Chose the Nails

He Is Your God

"I am God and not a human;
I am the Holy One, and I am among you."

Before you read any further, reflect on those last four words, "I am among you." Do you believe that? Do you believe God is near? He wants you to. He wants you to know he is in the midst of your world. Wherever you are as you read these words, he is present. In your car. On the plane. In your office, your bedroom, your den. He's near.

God is in the thick of things in your world. He has not taken up residence in a distant galaxy. He has not removed himself from history. He has not chosen to seclude himself on a throne in an incandescent castle.

He has drawn near. He has involved himself in the carpools, heartbreaks, and funeral homes of our day. He is as near to us on Monday as on Sunday. In the schoolroom as in the sanctuary. At the coffee break as much as the communion table.

And the Angels Were Silent

God's Greatest Blessings

The Son of Man will die, just as the Scriptures say.

MATTHEW 26:24

God's greatest blessings often come costumed as disasters. Any doubters need to do nothing more than ascend the hill of Calvary.

Jerusalem's collective opinion that Friday was this: Jesus is finished. What other conclusion made sense? The religious leaders had turned him in. Rome had refused to bail him out. His followers had tucked their tails and scattered. He was nailed to a cross and left to die, which he did. They silenced his lips, sealed his tomb, and, as any priest worth the price of a phylactery would tell you, Jesus is history. Three years of power and promises are decomposing in a borrowed grave. Search the crucifixion sky for one ray of hope, and you won't find it.

Such is the view of the disciples, the opinion of the friends, and the outlook of the enemies.

But God is not surprised. His plan is right on schedule. Even in—especially in—death, Christ is still the king, the king over his own crucifixion.

Next Door Savior

God Loves to Surprise Us

People receive God's promises by having faith.
This happens so the promise can be a free gift.

ROMANS 4:16

Our problem is not so much that God doesn't give us what we hope for as it is that we don't know the right thing for which to hope. (You may want to read that sentence again.)

Hope is not what you expect; it is what you would never dream. It is a wild, improbable tale with a pinch-me-I'm-dreaming ending. It's Abraham adjusting his bifocals so he can see not his grandson, but his son. It's Moses standing in the promised land not with Aaron or Miriam at his side, but with Elijah and the transfigured Christ. . . .

Hope is not a granted wish or a favor performed; no, it is far greater than that. It is a zany, unpredictable dependence on a God who loves to surprise us out of our socks and be there in the flesh to see our reaction.

God Came Near

Designed by God

*If anyone ministers, let him do it
as with the ability which God supplies.*

1 PETER 4:11 NKJV

God shaped you according to your purpose. How else can you explain yourself? Your ability to diagnose an engine problem by the noise it makes, to bake a cake without a recipe. You knew the Civil War better than your American history teacher. You know the name of every kid in the orphanage. How do you explain such quirks of skill?

God. He knew young Israel would need a code, so he gave Moses a love for the law. He knew the doctrine of grace would need a fiery advocate, so he set Paul ablaze. And in your case, he knew what your generation would need and gave it. He designed you. And *his design defines your destiny.* Remember Peter's admonition? "If anyone ministers, let him do it as with the ability which God supplies."

Cure for the Common Life

How Wide God's Love

For God so loved the world that
he gave his only begotten Son. . . .

As boldly as the center beam of the cross proclaims God's holiness, the crossbeam declares his love. And, oh, how wide his love reaches.

Aren't you glad the verse does not read:

"For God so loved the rich . . . "?

Or, "For God so loved the famous . . . "?

Or, "For God so loved the thin . . . "?

It doesn't. Nor does it state, "For God so loved the Europeans or Africans . . . " "the sober or successful . . . " "the young or the old . . . "

No, when we read John 3:16, we simply (and happily) read, "For God so loved the world."

How wide is God's love? Wide enough for the whole world.

He Chose the Nails

Peace Through Prayer

*God's peace . . . will keep your
hearts and minds in Christ Jesus.*

PHILIPPIANS 4:7

The worrisome heart pays a high price for doing so. *Worry* comes from the Greek word that means "to divide the mind." Anxiety splits us right down the middle, creating a double-minded thinker. Rather than take away tomorrow's trouble, worry voids today's strength. Perception is divided, distorting your vision. Strength is divided, wasting your energy. Who can afford to lose power?

But how can we stop doing so? Paul offers a two-pronged answer: God's part and our part. Our part includes prayer and gratitude. "Don't worry about anything; instead, *pray* about everything. Tell God what you need, and *thank him* for all he has done" (Phil. 4:6 NLT, emphasis mine).

God's part? "If you do this, you will experience God's peace, which is far more wonderful than the human mind can understand" (Phil. 4:7 NLT).

Come Thirsty

God's Testimony

The testimony of the LORD is sure,
making wise the simple.

PSALM 19:7 NKJV

A small seed becoming a towering tree.

A thin stalk pushing back the earth.

A rainbow arching in the midst of the thundercloud. . . .

"God's testimony," wrote David, "makes wise the simple."

God's testimony. When was the last time you witnessed it? A stroll through knee-high grass in a green meadow. An hour listening to seagulls or looking at seashells on the beach. Or witnessing the shafts of sunlight brighten the snow on a crisp winter dawn. . . .

There comes a time when we should lay down our pens and commentaries and step out of our offices and libraries. To really understand and believe in the miracle on the cross, we'd do well to witness God's miracles every day.

No Wonder They Call Him the Savior

Free to Enter His Presence

When Jesus had cried out again in a loud voice, he gave up his spirit. At that moment the curtain of the temple was torn in two from top to bottom.

MATTHEW 27:50–51 NIV

It's as if the hands of heaven had been gripping the veil, waiting for this moment. Keep in mind the size of the curtain—sixty feet tall and thirty feet wide. One instant it was whole; the next it was ripped in two from top to bottom. No delay. No hesitation.

What did the torn curtain mean? For the Jews it meant no more barrier between them and the Holy of Holies. No more priests to go between them and God. No more animal sacrifices to atone for their sins.

And for us? What did the torn curtain signify for us?

We are welcome to enter into God's presence— any day, any time. God has removed the barrier that separates us from him. The barrier of sin? Down. He has removed the curtain.

He Chose the Nails

Love Makes the Difference

*The person who is forgiven only
a little will love only a little.*

LUKE 7:47

We can replace the word *forgiven* with *accepted* and maintain the integrity of the passage. "He who is *accepted* little loves little." If we think God is harsh and unfair, guess how we'll treat people. Harshly and unfairly. But if we discover that God has doused us with unconditional love, would that make a difference?

The apostle Paul would say so! Talk about a turnaround. He went from bully to teddy bear. Paul B.C. (Before Christ) sizzled with anger. He "made havoc of the church" (Acts 8:3 NKJV). Paul A.D. (After Discovery) brimmed with love. . . .

His accusers beat him, stoned him, jailed him, mocked him. But can you find one occasion where he responded in kind? One temper tantrum? One angry outburst? *This is a different man.* His anger is gone. His passion is strong. His devotion is unquestioned. But rash outbursts of anger? A thing of the past.

What made the difference? He encountered Christ.

A Love Worth Giving

The Right Direction

You are like foreigners and strangers in this world.

1 PETER 2:11

Your Shepherd knows that you were not made for this place. He knows you are not equipped for this place. So he has come to guide you out.

He has come to restore your soul. He is the perfect one to do so.

He has the right vision. He reminds you that "you are like foreigners and strangers in this world." And he urges you to lift your eyes from the jungle around you to the heaven above you.

He also has the right direction. He made the boldest claim in the history of man when he declared, "I am the way" (John 14:6). People wondered if the claim was accurate. He answered their questions by cutting a path through the underbrush of sin and death . . . and escaping alive. He's the only One who ever did. And he is the only One who can help you and me do the same.

Traveling Light

Remember Jesus

*"Remember Jesus Christ, who was raised from the
dead. . . . This is the Good News I preach."*

In a letter written within earshot of the
sharpening of the blade that would sever
his head, Paul urged Timothy to remember.
You can almost picture the old warrior smiling as
he wrote the words. "Remember Jesus Christ,
who was raised from the dead. . . . This is the
Good News I preach." . . .

When times get hard, remember Jesus. When
people don't listen, remember Jesus. When tears
come, remember Jesus. When disappointment is
your bed partner, remember Jesus.

Remember holiness in tandem with humanity.
Remember the sick who were healed with callused
hands. Remember the dead called from the grave
with a Galilean accent. Remember the eyes of
God that wept human tears.

Six Hours One Friday

God's Family of Friends

*His unchanging plan has always been
to adopt us into his own family by bringing us
to himself through Jesus Christ.*

EPHESIANS 1:5 NLT

God offers you a family of friends and friends who are family—his church. When you transfer your trust into Christ, he not only pardons you; he places you in his family of friends.

"Family" far and away outpaces any other biblical term to describe the church. "Brothers" or "brothers and sisters" appears a whopping 148 times between the book of Acts and the book of Revelation.

God heals his family through his family. In the church we use our gifts to love each other, honor one another, keep an eye on troublemakers, and carry each other's burdens.

Cure for the Common Life

A Cloak of Love

Love . . . always protects.

1 CORINTHIANS 13:4–7 NIV

When Paul said, "Love always protects," he might have been thinking of a coat. One scholar thinks he was. *The Theological Dictionary of the New Testament* is known for its word study, not its poetry. But the scholar sounds poetic as he explains the meaning of *protect* as used in 1 Corinthians 13:7. The word conveys, he says, "the idea of covering with a cloak of love."

Remember receiving one? You were nervous about the test, but the teacher stayed late to help you. You were far from home and afraid, but your mother phoned to comfort you. You were innocent and accused, so your friend stood to defend you. Covered with encouragement. Covered with tender-hearted care. Covered with protection. *Covered with a cloak of love.*

A Love Worth Giving

What Is Grace?

> *My grace is enough for you.*
> *When you are weak, my power is made perfect in you.*
>
> 2 CORINTHIANS 12:9

 What is grace? It's what someone gives us
out of the goodness of his heart, not out of
the perfection of ours. The story of grace is the
good news that says that when we come, he gives.
That's what grace is. . . .

Grace is something you did not expect. It is
something you certainly could never earn. But
grace is something you'd never turn down.

You know what happens when someone sees
the grace of God? When someone really tastes the
forgiving and liberating grace of God? Some one
who tastes God's grace is the hardest worker,
the most morally pure individual, and the person
most willing to forgive.

The Inspirational Study Bible

Life Is Not Fair

Love your neighbor as you love yourself.

GALATIANS 5:14

As long as you hate your enemy, a jail door is closed and a prisoner is taken. But when you try to understand and release your foe from your hatred, then the prisoner is released and that prisoner is you.

Perhaps you don't like that idea. Perhaps the thought of forgiveness is unrealistic. Perhaps the idea of trying to understand the Judases in our world is simply too gracious.

My response to you then is a question. What do you suggest? Will harboring the anger solve the problem? Will getting even remove the hurt? Does hatred do any good? Again, I'm not minimizing your hurt or justifying their actions. But I am saying that justice won't come this side of eternity. And demanding that your enemy get his or her share of pain will, in the process, be most painful to you.

May I gently but firmly remind you of something you know but may have forgotten? Life is not fair. That's not pessimism; it's fact.

And the Angels Were Silent

Reliability

He who is faithful in what is least is faithful also in much.

There is a common denominator in any form of greatness—reliability.

It's the bread and butter characteristic of achievement. It's the shared ingredient behind retirement pens, Hall of Fame awards, and golden anniversaries. It is the quality that produces not momentary heroics but monumental lives.

The Bible has its share. . . . Consistent and predictable, these saints were spurred by a gut-level conviction that they had been called by no one less than God himself. As a result, their work wasn't affected by moods, cloudy days, or rocky trails. Their performance graph didn't rise and fall with roller-coaster irregularity. They weren't addicted to accolades or applause nor deterred by grumpy bosses or empty wallets. . . . And since their loyalty was not determined by their comfort, they were just as faithful in dark prisons as they were in spotlighted pulpits.

God Came Near

Hear His Music

The Lord disciplines those he loves.

HEBREWS 12:6

Oh, how God wants you to hear his music.
He has a rhythm that will race your
heart and lyrics that will stir your tears. You want
to journey to the stars? He can take you there.
You want to lie down in peace? His music can
soothe your soul.

But first, he's got to get rid of that country-
western stuff. (Forgive me, Nashville. Only an
example.)

And so he begins tossing the CDs. A friend
turns away. The job goes bad. Your spouse doesn't
understand. The church is dull. One by one he
removes the options until all you have left is God.

He would do that? Absolutely. If he must
silence every voice, he will. He wants you to hear
his music.

Traveling Light

Loved by God

The LORD loves you.

DEUTERONOMY 7:8 NLT

God loves you simply because he has chosen to do so.

He loves you when you don't feel lovely.

He loves you when no one else loves you. Others may abandon you, divorce you, and ignore you, but God will love you. Always. No matter what.

This is his sentiment: "I'll call nobodies and make them somebodies; I'll call the unloved and make them beloved" (Rom. 9:25 MSG).

This is his promise. "I have loved you, my people, with an everlasting love. With unfailing love I have drawn you to myself" (Jer. 31:3 NLT).

Do you know what else that means? You have a deep aquifer of love from which to draw. When you find it hard to love, then you need a drink! Drink deeply! Drink daily!

A Love Worth Giving

"You Are Mine"

Our lives are in the True One and in his Son, Jesus Christ.

1 JOHN 5:20

God knows your entire story, from first word to final breath, and with clear assessment declares, "You are mine."

My publisher made a similar decision with this book. Before agreeing to publish it, they read it—every single word. Multiple sets of editorial eyes scoured the manuscript, moaning at my bad jokes, grading my word crafting, suggesting a tune-up here and a tone-down there. We volleyed pages back and forth, writer to editor to writer, until finally we all agreed—this is it. It's time to publish or pass. The publisher could pass, mind you. Sometimes they do. But in this case, obviously they didn't. With perfect knowledge of this imperfect product, they signed on. What you read may surprise you, but not them.

What you do may stun you, but not God. With perfect knowledge of your imperfect life, God signed on.

Come Thirsty

Love the Overlooked

Put on the apron of humility, to serve one another.

1 PETER 5:5 TEV

Servanthood requires no unique skill or seminary degree. Regardless of your strengths, training, or church tenure, you can . . . love the overlooked.

Jesus sits in your classroom, wearing the thick glasses, outdated clothing, and a sad face. You've seen him. He's Jesus.

Jesus works in your office. Pregnant again, she shows up to work late and tired. No one knows the father. According to water-cooler rumors, even she doesn't know the father. You've seen her. She's Jesus.

When you talk to the lonely student, befriend the weary mom, you love Jesus. He dresses in the garb of the overlooked and ignored. "Whenever you did one of these things to someone overlooked or ignored, that was me— you did it to me" (Matt. 25:40 MSG).

Cure for the Common Life

April

The Lord is my shepherd;
I have everything I need.

—Psalm 23:1

God's Name

The LORD is my shepherd; I have everything I need.

PSALM 23:1

"You want to know who God really is?" David asks. "Then read this." And he writes the name *Yahweh*. "Yahweh is my shepherd."

Though foreign to us, the name was rich to David. So rich, in fact, that David chose *Yahweh* over *El Shaddai* (God Almighty), *El Elyon* (God Most High), and *El Olam* (God the Everlasting). These and many other titles for God were at David's disposal. But when he considered all the options, David chose *Yahweh*.

Why *Yahweh?* Because *Yahweh* is God's name. You can call me preacher or writer or half-baked golfer—these are accurate descriptions, but these aren't my names. I might call you dad, mom, doctor, or student, and those terms may describe you, but they aren't your name. If you want to call me by my name, say *Max*. If I call you by your name, I say it. And if you want to call God by his name, say *Yahweh*.

Traveling Light

A Man of Sorrows

He is despised and rejected by men,
a Man of sorrows and acquainted with grief.

ISAIAH 53:3 NKJV

The scene is very simple; you'll recognize it quickly. A grove of twisted olive trees. Ground cluttered with large rocks. A low stone fence. A dark, dark night. . . .

See that solitary figure? . . . Flat on the ground. Face stained with dirt and tears. Fists pounding the hard earth. Eyes wide with a stupor of fear. Hair matted with salty sweat. Is that blood on his forehead?

That's Jesus. Jesus in the Garden of Gethsemane. . . .

We see an agonizing, straining, and struggling Jesus. We see a "man of sorrows." We see a man struggling with fear, wrestling with commitments, and yearning for relief.

Seeing God like this does wonders for our own suffering. God was never more human than at this hour. God was never nearer to us than when he hurt. The Incarnation was never so fulfilled as in the garden.

No Wonder They Call Him the Savior

Patience Freely Offered

The Spirit produces the fruit of love, joy, peace, patience.

GALATIANS 5:22

If you find patience hard to give, you might ask this question. How infiltrated are you with God's patience? You've heard about it. Read about it. Perhaps underlined Bible passages regarding it. But have you received it? The proof is in your patience. Patience deeply received results in patience freely offered. . . .

God does more than demand patience from us; he offers it to us. Patience is a fruit of his Spirit. It hangs from the tree of Galatians 5:22: "The Spirit produces the fruit of love, joy, peace, patience." Have you asked God to give you some fruit? *Well I did once, but* . . . But what? Did you, h'm, grow impatient? Ask him again and again and again. He won't grow impatient with your pleading, and you will receive patience in your praying.

A Love Worth Giving

God's Work of Art

We are God's masterpiece.

EPHESIANS 2:10 NLT

Over a hundred years ago, a group of fishermen were relaxing in a Scottish seaside inn. One of the men gestured widely and his arm struck the serving maid's tea tray, sending the teapot flying into the whitewashed wall. The innkeeper surveyed the damage and sighed, "The whole wall will have to be repainted."

"Perhaps not," offered a stranger. "Let me work with it."

Having nothing to lose, the proprietor consented. The man pulled pencils, brushes, and pigment out of an art box. . . . In time, an image began to emerge: a stag with a great rack of antlers. The man inscribed his signature at the bottom, paid for his meal, and left. His name: Sir Edwin Landseer, famous painter of wildlife.

In his hands, a mistake became a masterpiece. God's hands do the same, over and over. He draws together the disjointed blotches in our life and renders them an expression of his love.

Come Thirsty

A Clear Vision of the Cross

Christ died for sins once for all, the righteous
for the unrighteous, to bring you to God.

1 PETER 3:18 NIV

One of the reference points of London is the Charing Cross. It is near the geographical center of the city and serves as a navigational tool for those confused by the streets.

A little girl was lost in the great city. A policeman found her. Between sobs and tears, she explained she didn't know her way home. He asked her if she knew her address. She didn't. He asked her phone number; she didn't know that either. But when he asked her what she knew, suddenly her face lit up.

"I know the Cross," she said. "Show me the Cross and I can find my way home from there."

So can you. Keep a clear vision of the cross on your horizon and you can find your way home.

And the Angels Were Silent

You are *You-Nique*

Each of us is an original.

GALATIANS 5:26 MSG

God made you *you-nique*.

Secular thinking, as a whole, doesn't buy this. Secular society sees no author behind the book, no architect behind the house, no purpose behind or beyond life. It simply says, "You can be anything you want to be."

Be a butcher if you want to, a sales rep if you like. Be an ambassador if you really care. You can be anything you want to be. But can you? If God didn't pack within you the meat sense of a butcher, the people skills of a salesperson, or the world vision of an ambassador, can you be one? An unhappy, dissatisfied one perhaps. But a fulfilled one? No. Can an acorn become a rose, a whale fly like a bird, or lead become gold? Absolutely not. You cannot be anything you want to be. But you can be everything God wants you to be.

Cure for the Common Life

He Walked Among Us

*We do not have a high priest who is
unable to sympathize with our weaknesses.*

HEBREWS 4:15

When God chose to reveal himself, he did
so (surprise of surprises) through a human
body. The tongue that called forth the dead was a
human one. The hand that touched the leper had
dirt under its nails. The feet upon which the
woman wept were calloused and dusty. And his
tears . . . oh, don't miss the tears . . . they came from
a heart as broken as yours or mine ever has been.

"For we do not have a high priest who is
unable to sympathize with our weaknesses."

So, people came to him. My, how they came
to him! They came at night; they touched him as
he walked down the street; they followed him
around the sea; they invited him into their
homes and placed their children at his feet. Why?
Because he refused to be a statue in a cathedral or
a priest in an elevated pulpit. He chose instead to
be Jesus.

God Came Near

Try Again

"We worked hard all night and caught nothing."

LUKE 5:5 NASB

Do you have any worn, wet, empty nets?

Do you know the feeling of a sleepless, fishless night? Of course you do. For what have you been casting?

Solvency? "My debt is an anvil around my neck . . ."

Faith? "I want to believe, but . . ."

Healing? "I've been sick so long . . ."

A happy marriage? "No matter what I do . . ."

I've worked hard all night and caught nothing.

You've felt what Peter felt. You've sat where Peter sat. And now Jesus is asking you to go fishing. He knows your nets are empty. He knows your heart is weary. He knows you'd like nothing more than to turn your back on the mess and call it a life.

But he urges, "It's not too late to try again."

See if Peter's reply won't help you formulate your own. "I will do as You say and let down the nets" (v. 5).

Next Door Savior

Our Middle C

I the LORD do not change.

MALACHI 3:6

When Lloyd Douglas, author of *The Robe* and other novels, attended college, he lived in a boardinghouse. A retired, wheelchair-bound music professor resided on the first floor. Each morning Douglas would stick his head in the door of the teacher's apartment and ask the same question, "Well, what's the good news?" The old man would pick up his tuning fork, tap it on the side of the wheelchair, and say, "That's middle C! It was middle C yesterday; it will be middle C tomorrow; it will be middle C a thousand years from now. The tenor upstairs sings flat. The piano across the hall is out of tune, but, my friend, that is middle C."

You and I need a middle C. Haven't you had enough change in your life? Relationships change. Health changes. The weather changes. But the Yahweh who ruled the earth last night is the same Yahweh who rules it today. Same convictions. Same plan. Same mood. Same love. He never changes.

Traveling Light

Be Kind to Yourself

*Be kind to one another, tenderhearted, forgiving one
another, even as God in Christ forgave you.*

EPHESIANS 4:32 NKJV

Our heavenly Father is kind to us. And
since he is so kind to us, can't we be a little
kinder to ourselves? *Oh, but you don't know me,
Max. You don't know my faults and my thoughts.
You don't know the gripes I grumble and the
complaints I mumble.* No, I don't, but he does.
He knows everything about you, yet he doesn't
hold back his kindness toward you. Has he,
knowing all your secrets, retracted one promise
or reclaimed one gift?

No, he is kind to you. Why don't you be
kind to yourself? He forgives your faults. Why
don't you do the same? He thinks tomorrow is
worth living. Why don't you agree? He believes
in you enough to call you his ambassador, his
follower, even his child. Why not take his cue and
believe in yourself?

A Love Worth Giving

Made in His Image

Then God said, "Let Us make man in Our image."

GENESIS 1:26 NKJV

Imagine God's creativity. Of all we don't know about the creation, there is one thing we do know—he did it with a smile. He must've had a blast. Painting the stripes on the zebra, hanging the stars in the sky, putting the gold in the sunset. What creativity! Stretching the neck of the giraffe, putting the flutter in the mockingbird's wings, planting the giggle in the hyena.

What a time he had. Like a whistling carpenter in his workshop, he loved every bit of it. He poured himself into the work. So intent was his creativity that he took a day off at the end of the week just to rest.

And then, as a finale to a brilliant performance, he made man. With his typical creative flair, he began with a useless mound of dirt and ended up with an invaluable species called a human. A human who had the unique honor to bear the stamp, "In His Image."

No Wonder They Call Him the Savior

God Gets Into Our Lives

I do not live anymore—it is Christ who lives in me.

GALATIANS 2:20

You have leaves to rake. A steering wheel to grip. A neighbor's hand to shake. Simply put, you have things to do.

So does God. Babies need hugs. Children need good-night tucks. AIDS orphans need homes. Stressed-out executives need hope. God has work to do. And he uses our hands to do it.

What the hand is to the glove, the Spirit is to the Christian. . . . God gets into us. At times, imperceptibly. Other times, disruptively. God gets his fingers into our lives, inch by inch reclaiming the territory that is rightfully his.

Your tongue. He claims it for his message.

Your feet. He requisitions them for his purpose.

Your mind? He made it and intends to use it for his glory.

Your eyes, face, and hands? Through them he will weep, smile, and touch.

Come Thirsty

A Good Choice

*Let us come near to God with a
sincere heart and a sure faith.*

HEBREWS 10:22

It would have been nice if God had let us
order life like we order a meal. I'll take good
health and a high IQ. I'll pass on the music skills,
but give me a fast metabolism. . . . Would've been
nice. But it didn't happen. When it came to your
life on earth, you weren't given a voice or a vote.

But when it comes to life after death, you
were. In my book that seems like a good deal.
Wouldn't you agree? . . .

Have we been given any greater privilege
than that of choice? Not only does this privilege
offset any injustice, the gift of free will can offset
any mistakes.

You've made some bad choices in life, haven't
you? You've chosen the wrong friends, maybe the
wrong career, even the wrong spouse. You look
back over your life and say, "If only . . . if only I
could make up for those bad choices." You can.
One good choice for eternity offsets a thousand
bad ones on earth.

The choice is yours.

He Chose the Nails

It's Up to You

"Behold, I stand at the door, and knock: if any man hear my voice, and open the door, I will come in to him."

REVELATION 3:20 KJV

Perhaps you've seen Holman Hunt's painting of Jesus. Stone archway . . . ivy-covered bricks . . . Jesus standing before a heavy wooden door.

It was in a Bible I often held as a young boy. Beneath the painting were the words, "Behold, I stand at the door, and knock: if any man hear my voice, and open the door, I will come in to him."

Years later I read about a surprise in the painting. Holman Hunt had intentionally left out something that only the most careful eye would note as missing. I had not noticed it. When I was told about it I went back and looked. Sure enough, it wasn't there. There was no doorknob on the door. It could be opened only from the inside. . . .

God comes to your house, steps up to the door, and knocks. But it's up to you to let him in.

And the Angels Were Silent

The Empty Tomb

"He has been raised from the dead. . . .
Come, see where his body was lying."

MATTHEW 28:6 NLT

Following Christ demands faith, but not blind faith. "Come and see," the angel invites. Shall we?

Take a look at the vacated tomb. Did you know the opponents of Christ never challenged its vacancy? No Pharisee or Roman soldier ever led a contingent back to the burial site and declared, "The angel was wrong. The body is here. It was all a rumor."

They would have if they could have. Within weeks disciples occupied every Jerusalem street corner, announcing a risen Christ. What quicker way for the enemies of the church to shut them up than to produce a cold and lifeless body? But they had no cadaver to display.

Helps explain the Jerusalem revival. When the apostles argued for the empty tomb, the people looked to the Pharisees for a rebuttal. But they had none to give. As A. M. Fairbairn put it long ago, "The silence of the Jews is as eloquent as the speech of the Christians!"

Next Door Savior

Eternal Instants

You have done good things for your servant,
as you have promised, LORD.

PSALM 119:65

Eternal instants. You've had them. We all have.

Sharing a porch swing on a summer evening with your grandchild.

Seeing her face in the glow of a candle.

Putting your arm into your husband's as you stroll through the golden leaves and breathe the brisk autumn air.

Listening to your six-year-old thank God for everything from goldfish to Grandma.

Such moments are necessary because they remind us that everything is okay. The King is still on the throne and life is still worth living. Eternal instants remind us that love is still the greatest possession and the future is nothing to fear.

The next time an instant in your life begins to be eternal, let it.

God Came Near

There's Only One You

*From the place of His dwelling He looks on
all the inhabitants of the earth;
He fashions their hearts individually.*

PSALM 33:14–15

You are the only you God made.
He made you and broke the mold. . . .
Every single baby is a brand-new idea from the
mind of God.

No one can duplicate your life. Scan history
for your replica; you won't find it. God tailor-made
you. He "personally formed and made each one"
(Isa. 43:7 MSG). No box of "backup yous" sits in
God's workshop. You aren't one of many bricks in
the mason's pile or one of a dozen bolts in the
mechanic's drawer. You are it! And if you aren't
you, we don't get you. The world misses out.

You are heaven's Halley's comet; we have one
shot at seeing you shine.

Cure for the Common Life

The Shadow of the Cross

God put on him the wrong who never did anything wrong, so we could be put right with God.

2 CORINTHIANS 5:21 MSG

Envision the moment. God on his throne. You on the earth. And between you and God, suspended between you and heaven, is Christ on his cross. Your sins have been placed on Jesus. God, who punishes sin, releases his rightful wrath on your mistakes. Jesus receives the blow. Since Christ is between you and God, you don't. The sin is punished, but you are safe—safe in the shadow of the cross.

This is what God did, but why, why would he do it? Moral duty? Heavenly obligation? Paternal requirement? No. God is required to do nothing.

The reason for the cross? God loves the world.

He Chose the Nails

Pray About Everything

Call to me in times of trouble.
I will save you, and you will honor me.

PSALM 50:15

Want to worry less? Then pray more.
Rather than look forward in fear, look
upward in faith. This command surprises no one.
Regarding prayer, the Bible never blushes. Jesus
taught people that "it was necessary for them to
pray consistently and never quit" (Luke 18:1 MSG).
Paul told believers, "Devote yourselves to prayer
with an alert mind and a thankful heart"
(Col. 4:2 NLT). James declared, "Are any among
you suffering? They should keep on praying about
it" (James 5:13 NLT).

Rather than worry about anything, "pray
about everything." Everything? Diaper changes
and dates? Business meetings and broken
bathtubs? Procrastinations and prognostications?
Pray about everything.

Come Thirsty

Covered with Christ

Your life is now hidden with Christ in God.

COLOSSIANS 3:3 NIV

The Chinese language has a great symbol for the truth of that verse. The word for *righteousness* is a combination of two pictures. On the top is a lamb. Beneath the lamb is a person. The lamb covers the person. Isn't that the essence of righteousness? The Lamb of Christ over the child of God? Whenever the Father looks down on you, what does he see? He sees his Son, the perfect Lamb of God, hiding you. Christians are like their ancestor Abel. We come to God by virtue of the flock. Cain came with the work of his own hands. God turned him away. Abel came, and we come, dependent upon the sacrifice of the Lamb, and we are accepted. Like the Chinese symbol, we are covered by the lamb, hidden in Christ.

When God looks at you, he doesn't see you; he sees Jesus. And how does he respond when he sees Jesus? He rends the heavens and vibrates the earth with the shout, "You are my Son, whom I love, and I am very pleased with you" (Mark 1:11).

A Love Worth Giving

He Gives Us Himself

"I am with you always, to the very end of the age."

MATTHEW 28:20 NIV

The story is told of a man on an African safari deep in the jungle. The guide before him had a machete and was whacking away the tall weeds and thick underbrush. The traveler, wearied and hot, asked in frustration, "Where are we? Do you know where you are taking me? Where is the path?!" The seasoned guide stopped and looked back at the man and replied, "I am the path."

We ask the same questions, don't we? We ask God, "Where are you taking me? Where is the path?" And he, like the guide, doesn't tell us. Oh, he may give us a hint or two, but that's all. If he did, would we understand? Would we comprehend our location? No, like the traveler, we are unacquainted with this jungle. So rather than give us an answer, Jesus gives us a far greater gift. He gives us himself.

Traveling Light

Jesus Offers Peace

"Peace be with you."

JOHN 20:19

The church of Jesus Christ began with a group of frightened men in a second-floor room in Jerusalem.

Though they'd marched with Jesus for three years, they now sat . . . afraid. They were timid soldiers, reluctant warriors, speechless messengers.

Daring to dream that the master had left them some word, some plan, some direction, they came back.

But little did they know their wildest dream wasn't wild enough. Just as someone mumbles, "It's no use," they hear a noise. They hear a voice: "Peace be with you."

The one betrayed sought his betrayers. What did he say to them? Not "What a bunch of flops!" Not "I told you so." No "Where-were-you-when-I-needed-you?" speeches. But simply one phrase, "Peace be with you." The very thing they didn't have was the very thing he offered: peace.

Six Hours One Friday

We Are Family

Be devoted to one another in brotherly love.

ROMANS 12:10 NIV

Common belief identifies members of God's family. And common affection unites them. Paul gives this relationship rule for the church: "Be devoted to one another in brotherly love." The apostle plays the wordsmith here, bookending the verse with fraternal-twin terms. He begins with *philostorgos* (*philos* means friendly; *storgos* means family love) and concludes with *philadelphia* (*phileo* means tender affection; *adelphia* means brethren). An awkward but accurate translation of the verse might be "Have a friend/family devotion to each other in a friend/family sort of way." If Paul doesn't get us with the first adjective, he catches us with the second. In both he reminds us: the church is God's family.

You didn't pick me. I didn't pick you. You may not like me. I may not like you. But since God picked and likes us both, we are family.

Cure for the Common Life

Love Protects

The LORD God made clothes from animal skins
for the man and his wife and dressed them.

GENESIS 3:21

That simple sentence suggests three powerful scenes.

Scene 1: God slays an animal. For the first time in the history of the earth, dirt is stained with blood. Innocent blood. The beast committed no sin. The creature did not deserve to die.

Adam and Eve did. The couple deserve to die, but they live. . . .

Scene 2: Clothing is made. The shaper of the stars now becomes a tailor.

And in Scene 3: God dresses them. "The Lord . . . dressed them."

Adam and Eve are on their way out of the garden. They've been told to leave, but now God tells them to stop. "Those fig leaves," he says, shaking his head, "will never do." And he produces some clothing. But he doesn't throw the garments at their feet and tell them to get dressed. He dresses them himself. As a father would zip up the jacket of a preschooler. God covers them.

A Love Worth Giving

A Plea for Help

"We are getting what we deserve.
This man has done nothing wrong."

LUKE 23:41 TLB

We are guilty and he is innocent.

We are filthy and he is pure.

We are wrong and he is right.

He is not on that cross for his sins. He is there for ours.

And once the crook understands this, his request seems only natural. As he looks into the eyes of his last hope, he makes the same request any Christian has made: "Remember me when you come into your kingdom" (Luke 23:42 TLB).

No stained-glass homilies. No excuses. Just a desperate plea for help.

At this point Jesus performs the greatest miracle of the cross. Greater than the earthquake. Greater than the tearing of the temple curtain. . . .

He performs the miracle of forgiveness: "Today you will be with me in Paradise. This is a solemn promise" (Luke 23:43 TLB).

Six Hours One Friday

Think of Home

When you have many kinds of troubles, you should be full of joy, because you know that these troubles test your faith, and this will give you patience.

JAMES 1:2

God didn't say, "*If* you have many kinds of troubles" . . . he said, "*When* you have many kinds of troubles . . ." Troubles are part of the package. Betrayals are part of our troubles. Don't be surprised when betrayals come. Don't look for fairness here—look instead where Jesus looked.

While going through hell, Jesus kept his eyes on heaven. While surrounded by enemies he kept his mind on his father. While abandoned on earth, he kept his heart on home. "In the future you will see the Son of Man sitting at the right hand of God, the Powerful One, and coming on clouds in the sky" (Matt. 26:64).

When all of earth turns against you, all of heaven turns toward you. To keep your balance in a crooked world, . . . think of home.

And the Angels Were Silent

Thank You

Oh, love the LORD, all you His saints!
For the LORD preserves the faithful.

PSALM 31:23 NKJV

Re-liable. *Liable* means responsible. *Re* means over and over again.

I'm wondering if this book has found its way into the hands of some contemporary saints of reliability. If such is the case I can't resist the chance to say one thing.

Thank you.

Thank you, senior saints, for a generation of prayer and forest clearing.

Thank you, teachers, for the countless Sunday school lessons, prepared and delivered with tenderness.

Thank you, missionaries, for your bravery in sharing the timeless truth in a foreign tongue.

Thank you, preachers. You thought we weren't listening, but we were. And your stubborn sowing of God's seed is bearing fruit you may never see this side of the great harvest.

God Came Near

Never Alone

"I will . . . not forsake My people."

1 KINGS 6:13 NKJV

The Lord is with us. And, since the Lord is near, everything is different. Everything!

You may be facing death, but you aren't facing death alone; the Lord is with you. You may be facing unemployment, but you aren't facing unemployment alone; the Lord is with you. You may be facing marital struggles, but you aren't facing them alone; the Lord is with you. You may be facing debt, but you aren't facing debt alone; the Lord is with you.

Underline these words: *You are not alone.*

Your family may turn against you, but God won't. Your friends may betray you, but God won't. You may feel alone in the wilderness, but you are not. He is with you.

Traveling Light

Words of Strength

When you talk, do not say harmful things,
but say what people need—
words that will help others become stronger.

EPHESIANS 4:29

Before you speak, ask: Will what I'm about to say help others become stronger? You have the ability, with your words, to make a person stronger. Your words are to their soul what a vitamin is to their body. If you had food and saw someone starving, would you not share it? If you had water and saw someone dying of thirst, would you not give it? Of course you would. Then won't you do the same for their hearts? Your words are food and water!

Do not withhold encouragement from the discouraged.

Do not keep affirmation from the beaten down!

Speak words that make people stronger. Believe in them as God has believed in you.

A Love Worth Giving

He Knows How You Feel

He is able . . . to run to the cry of . . .
those who are being tempted and tested and tried.

HEBREWS 2:18 AMP

Jesus was angry enough to purge the temple, hungry enough to eat raw grain, distraught enough to weep in public, fun loving enough to be called a drunkard, winsome enough to attract kids, weary enough to sleep in a storm-bounced boat, poor enough to sleep on dirt and borrow a coin for a sermon illustration, radical enough to get kicked out of town, responsible enough to care for his mother, tempted enough to know the smell of Satan, and fearful enough to sweat blood.

But why? Why would heaven's finest Son endure earth's toughest pain? So you would know that "he is able . . . to run to the cry of . . . those who are being tempted and tested and tried."

Whatever you are facing, he knows how you feel.

Next Door Savior

May

Accept teaching from his mouth,
and keep his words in your heart.

—Job 22:22

Saturated in Love

Where God's love is there is no fear,
because God's perfect love drives out fear.

1 JOHN 4:18

We fear rejection, so we follow the crowd.
We fear not fitting in, so we take the drugs.
For fear of standing out, we wear what everyone
else wears. For fear of blending in, we wear what
no one else wears. For fear of sleeping alone, we
sleep with anyone. For fear of not being loved,
we search for love in all the wrong places.

But God flushes those fears. Those saturated in
God's love don't sell out to win the love of others.
They don't even sell out to win the love of God.

Do you think you need to? Do you think,
If I cuss less, pray more, drink less, study more . . .
if I try harder, God will love me more? Sniff
and smell Satan's stench behind those words.
We all need improvement, but we don't need
to woo God's love. We change because we
already have God's love. God's perfect love.

Come Thirsty

Wounded by Words

When they hurled their insults at him,
he did not retaliate.

1 PETER 2:23 NIV

Someone you love or respect slams you to the floor with a slur or slip of the tongue. And there you lie, wounded and bleeding. Perhaps the words were intended to hurt you, perhaps not; but that doesn't matter. The wound is deep. The injuries are internal. Broken heart, wounded pride, bruised feelings.

If you have suffered or are suffering because of someone else's words, you'll be glad to know that there is a balm for this laceration. Meditate on these words from 1 Peter 2:23: "When they hurled their insults at him, he did not retaliate. . . . Instead, he entrusted himself to him who judges justly."

Did you see what Jesus did? . . . He left the judging to God. He did not take on the task of seeking revenge. He demanded no apology. . . . He, to the astounding contrary, spoke on their defense. "Father, forgive them, for they do not know what they are doing" (Luke 23:34 NIV).

No Wonder They Call Him the Savior

Following Our Own Paths

All of us have strayed away like sheep.
We have left God's paths to follow our own.

ISAIAH 53:6 NLT

Adam and Eve turned their heads toward the hiss of the snake and for the first time ignored God. Eve did not ask, "God, what do you want?" Adam didn't suggest, "Let's consult the Creator." They acted as if they had no heavenly Father. His will was ignored, and sin, with death on its coattails, entered the world.

Sin sees the world with no God in it.

Where we might think of sin as slip-ups or missteps, God views sin as a godless attitude that leads to godless actions. "All of us have strayed away like sheep. We have left God's paths to follow our own." The sinful mind dismisses God. His counsel goes unconsulted. His opinion, unsolicited. . . .

The lack of God-centeredness leads to self-centeredness. Sin celebrates its middle letter—sIn.

Come Thirsty

The Language God Speaks

Accept teaching from his mouth,
and keep his words in your heart.

JOB 22:22

There is no language God will not speak. Which leads us to a delightful question. What language is he speaking to you? I'm not referring to an idiom or dialect but to the day-to-day drama of your life. . . .

There are times he speaks the "language of abundance." Is your tummy full? Are your bills paid? Got a little jingle in your pocket? Don't be so proud of what you have that you miss what you need to hear. Could it be you have much so you can give much?

Or how about the "language of affliction"? Talk about an idiom we avoid. But you and I both know how clearly God speaks in hospital hallways and sickbeds.

God speaks all languages—including yours. . . . What language is God speaking to you?

He Chose the Nails

A Hardy Faith

There is joy in the presence of the angels of God
when one sinner changes his heart and life.

LUKE 15:10

Our faith is not in religion; our faith is in God. A hardy, daring faith that believes God will do what is right, every time. And that God will do what it takes—whatever it takes—to bring his children home.

He is the shepherd in search of his lamb. His legs are scratched, his feet are sore and his eyes are burning. He scales the cliffs and traverses the fields. He explores the caves. He cups his hands to his mouth and calls into the canyon.

And the name he calls is yours.

He is the housewife in search of the lost coin. No matter that he has nine others, he won't rest until he has found the tenth. He searches the house. He moves furniture. . . . All other tasks can wait. Only one matters. The coin is of great value to him. He owns it. He will not stop until he finds it.

The coin he seeks is you.

And the Angels Were Silent

Heaven Came Down

*I have come down from heaven, not to do
My own will, but the will of Him who sent Me.*

JOHN 6:38

This is no run-of-the-mill messiah. His story was extraordinary. He called himself divine, yet allowed a minimum-wage Roman soldier to drive a nail into his wrist. He demanded purity, yet stood for the rights of a repentant whore. He called men to march, yet refused to allow them to call him King. He sent men into all the world, yet equipped them with only bended knees and memories of a resurrected carpenter.

Has it been a while since you have seen him? If your prayers seem stale, it probably has. If your faith seems to be trembling, perhaps your vision of him has blurred. If you can't find power to face your problems, perhaps it is time to face him.

One warning. Something happens to a person who has witnessed His Majesty. . . . One glimpse of the King and you are consumed by a desire to see more of him and say more about him.

God Came Near

God Is Uncaused

Remember that I am God, and there is no other God.
I am God, and there is no one like me.

No one breathed life into Yahweh. No one
sired him. No one gave birth to him.
No one caused him. No act brought him forth.

And since no act brought him forth, no act
can take him out. Does he fear an earthquake?
Does he tremble at a tornado? Hardly. Yahweh
sleeps through storms and calms the winds with
a word. Cancer does not trouble him, and
cemeteries do not disturb him. He was here
before they came. He'll be here after they are
gone. He is uncaused.

And he is ungoverned. Counselors can
comfort you *in* the storm, but you need a God
who can *still* the storm. Friends can hold your
hand at your deathbed, but you need a Yahweh
who has defeated the grave. Philosophers can
debate the meaning of life, but you need a Lord
who can declare the meaning of life.

Traveling Light

No Pecking Orders

*He humbled himself and became obedient
to death—even death on a cross!*

PHILIPPIANS 2:8 NIV

Jesus blasts the top birds of the church,
those who roost at the top of the spiritual
ladder and spread their plumes of robes, titles,
jewelry, and choice seats. Jesus won't stand for
it. It's easy to see why. How can I love others if
my eyes are only on me? How can I point to
God if I'm pointing at me? And, worse still,
how can someone see God if I keep fanning my
own tail feathers?

Jesus has no room for pecking orders. Love
"does not boast, it is not proud" (1 Cor. 13:4 NIV).

His solution to man-made caste systems? A
change of direction. In a world of upward mobility,
choose downward servility. Go down, not up.
"Regard one another as more important than
yourselves" (Phil. 2:3 NASB). That's what Jesus did.

He flip-flopped the pecking order. While
others were going up, he was going down. "He
humbled himself and became obedient to death—
even death on a cross!"

A Love Worth Giving

Forgiveness Follows Failure

*In the past God spoke . . . many times
and in many different ways. But now . . .
God has spoken to us through his Son.*

HEBREWS 1:1–2

God, motivated by love and directed by
divinity, surprised everyone. He became a
man. In an untouchable mystery, he disguised
himself as a carpenter and lived in a dusty
Judaean village. Determined to prove his love for
his creation, he walked incognito through his own
world. His callused hands touched wounds and
his compassionate words touched hearts. . . .

But as beautiful as this act of incarnation was,
it was not the zenith. Like a master painter God
reserved his masterpiece until the end. All the
earlier acts of love had been leading to this one.
The angels hushed and the heavens paused to
witness the finale. God unveils the canvas and the
ultimate act of creative compassion is revealed.

God on a cross. The Creator being sacrificed
for the creation. God convincing man once and
for all that forgiveness still follows failure.

No Wonder They Call Him the Savior

The Spirit's Work

If Christ is in you, then the Spirit gives you life.

ROMANS 8:10

Receiving the unseen is not easy. Most Christians find the cross of Christ easier to accept than the Spirit of Christ. Good Friday makes more sense than Pentecost. Christ, our substitute. Jesus taking our place. The Savior paying for our sins. These are astounding, yet embraceable, concepts. They fall in the arena of transaction and substitution, familiar territory for us. But Holy Spirit discussions lead us into the realm of the supernatural and unseen. We grow quickly quiet and cautious, fearing what we can't see or explain.

It helps to consider the Spirit's work from this angle. What Jesus did in Galilee is what the Holy Spirit does in us. Jesus dwelt among the people, teaching, comforting, and convicting. The Holy Spirit dwells within us, teaching, comforting, and convicting.

Come Thirsty

Uninterrupted Perfection

They divided his clothes among the four of them.
They also took his robe, but it was seamless,
woven in one piece from the top.

JOHN 19:23–24 NLT

It must have been Jesus' finest possession. Jewish tradition called for a mother to make such a robe and present it to her son as a departure gift when he left home. Had Mary done this for Jesus? We don't know. But we do know the tunic was without seam, woven from top to bottom. Why is this significant?

Scripture often describes our behavior as the clothes we wear. Peter urges us to be "clothed with humility" (1 Pet. 5:5 NKJV). David speaks of evil people who clothe themselves "with cursing" (Ps. 109:18 NKJV). Garments can symbolize character, and like his garment, Jesus' character was seamless. Coordinated. Unified. He was like his robe: uninterrupted perfection.

He Chose the Nails

The Invitation

All you who are thirsty, come and drink.

ISAIAH 55:1

To receive an invitation is to be honored—
to be held in high esteem. For that reason all
invitations deserve a kind and thoughtful response.

But the most incredible invitations are not
found in envelopes or fortune cookies, they are
found in the Bible. You can't read about God
without finding him issuing invitations. He
invited Eve to marry Adam, the animals to enter
the ark, David to be king, Israel to leave bondage,
Nehemiah to rebuild Jerusalem. God is an
inviting God. He invited Mary to birth his son,
the disciples to fish for men, the adulterous
woman to start over, and Thomas to touch his
wounds. God is the King who prepares the palace,
sets the table, and invites his subjects to come in.

God is a God who opens the door and waves
his hand pointing pilgrims to a full table.

His invitation is not just for a meal, however,
it is for life. An invitation to come into his
kingdom. . . . Who can come? Whoever wishes.

And the Angels Were Silent

Our Plight

When we were unable to help ourselves,
at the moment of our need, Christ died for us.

ROMANS 5:6

God did for us what I did for one of my
daughters in the shop at New York's
La Guardia Airport. The sign above the ceramic
pieces read Do Not Touch. But the wanting was
stronger than the warning, and she touched. And
it fell. By the time I looked up, ten-year-old Sara
was holding the two pieces of a New York City
skyline. Next to her was an unhappy store manager.
Over them both was the written rule. Between
them hung a nervous silence. My daughter had
no money. He had no mercy. So I stepped in.
"How much do we owe you?" I asked.

How was it that I owed anything? Simple. She
was my daughter. And since she could not pay, I did.

Since you and I cannot pay, Christ did.
We've broken so much more than souvenirs. We've
. . . broken God's heart.

With the law on the wall and shattered
commandments on the floor, Christ steps near
(like a neighbor) and offers a gift (like a Savior).

Next Door Savior

Seeing the Source

Whoever has seen me has seen the Father.

JOHN 14:9

Should a man see only popularity, he becomes a mirror, reflecting whatever needs to be reflected to gain acceptance. Though in vogue, he is vague. Though in style, he is stodgy. . . .

Should a man see only power, he becomes a wolf—prowling, hunting, and stalking the elusive game. Recognition is his prey and people are his prizes. His quest is endless. . . .

Should a man see only pleasure, he becomes a carnival thrill-seeker, alive only in bright lights, wild rides, and titillating entertainment. With lustful fever he races from ride to ride, satisfying his insatiable passion for sensations only long enough to look for another. . . .

Seekers of popularity, power, and pleasure. The end result is the same: painful unfulfillment.

Only in seeing his Maker does a man truly become man. For in seeing his Creator, man catches a glimpse of what he was intended to be.

God Came Near

Live Your Life

God, who makes everything work together,
will work you into his most excellent harmonies.

PHILIPPIANS 4:9 MSG

The Unseen Conductor prompts this orchestra we call living. When gifted teachers aid struggling students and skilled managers disentangle bureaucratic knots, when dog lovers love dogs and number crunchers zero balance the account, when you and I do the most what we do the best for the glory of God, we are "marvelously functioning parts in Christ's body" (Rom. 12:5 MSG).

You play no small part, because there is no small part to be played. "All of you together are Christ's body, and each one of you is a separate and necessary part of it" (1 Cor. 12:27 NLT). "Separate" and "necessary." Unique and essential. No one else has been given your lines. . . . The Author of the human drama entrusted your part to you alone. Live your life, or it won't be lived. We need you to be you.

You need you to be you.

Cure for the Common Life

No More Sacrifice

He came as High Priest of this better system which we now have.

HEBREWS 9:11 TLB

Even a casual student of Scripture notes the connection between blood and mercy. As far back as the son of Adam, worshipers knew "without the shedding of blood there is no forgiveness" (Heb. 9:22 NIV).

With a field as his temple and the ground as his altar, Abel became the first to do what millions would imitate. He offered a blood sacrifice for sins.

Those who followed suit form a long line: Abraham, Moses, Gideon, Samson, Saul, David. . . . They knew the shedding of blood was necessary for the forgiveness of sins. Jacob knew it too; hence, the stones were stacked for the altar. . . .

But the line ended at the cross. What Abel sought to accomplish in the field, God achieved with his Son. What Abel began, Christ completed. After Christ's sacrifice there would be no more need to shed blood.

He Chose the Nails

Perfect Peace

His peace will guard your hearts and minds as you live in Christ Jesus.

Believing prayer ushers in God's peace. Not a random, nebulous, earthly peace, but his peace. Imported from heaven. The same tranquility that marks the throne room, God offers to you.

Do you think he battles anxiety? You suppose he ever wrings his hands or asks the angels for antacids? Of course not. A problem is no more a challenge to God than a twig is to an elephant. God enjoys perfect peace because God enjoys perfect power.

And he offers his peace to you. A peace that will "guard your hearts and minds as you live in Christ Jesus." Paul employs a military metaphor here. The Philippians, living in a garrison town, were accustomed to the Roman sentries maintaining their watch. Before any enemy could get inside, he had to pass through the guards. God gives you the same offer. His supernatural peace overshadows you, . . . guarding your heart.

Come Thirsty

God's Open Arms

Keep your roots deep in him and
have your lives built on him.

COLOSSIANS 2:6

The people God used to change history were a ragbag of ne'er-do-wells and has-beens who found hope, not in their performance, but in God's proverbially open arms.

Let's start with Abraham. Though eulogized by Paul for his faith, this Father of a Nation wasn't without his weaknesses. He had a fibbing tongue that wouldn't stop! One time, in order to save his neck, he let the word get out that Sarah wasn't his wife but his sister, which was only half true. And then, not long later, he did it again! "And there Abraham said of his wife Sarah, 'She is my sister.'"

Twice he traded in his integrity for security. That's what you call confidence in God's promises? Can you build a nation on that kind of faith? God can. God took what was good and forgave what was bad and used "old forked tongue" to start a nation.

No Wonder They Call Him the Savior

Captured Thoughts

We capture every thought and make it give up and obey Christ.

2 CORINTHIANS 10:5

Capturing thoughts is serious business.

It was for Jesus. Remember the thoughts that came his way courtesy of the mouth of Peter? Jesus had just prophesied his death, burial, and resurrection, but Peter couldn't bear the thought of it. "Peter took Jesus aside and told him not to talk like that. . . . Jesus said to Peter, 'Go away from me, Satan! You are not helping me! You don't care about the things of God, but only about the things people think are important'" (Matt. 16:22–23).

See the decisiveness of Jesus? A trashy thought comes his way. He is tempted to entertain it. A cross-less life would be nice. But what does he do? He stands at the gangplank of the dock and says, "Get away from me." As if to say, "You are not allowed to enter my mind."

What if you did that. What if you took every thought captive?

A Love Worth Giving

God Is Righteous

He is gracious, and full of compassion, and righteous.

PSALM 112:4 NKJV

 Righteousness is who God is. God's righteousness "endures forever" (Ps. 112:3 NIV) and "reaches to the skies (Ps. 71:19 NIV).

God is righteous. His decrees are righteous (Rom. 1:32). His judgment is righteous (Rom. 2:5). His requirements are righteous (Rom. 8:4). His acts are righteous (Dan. 9:16). Daniel declared, "Our God is right in everything he does" (Dan. 9:14).

God is never wrong. He has never rendered a wrong decision, experienced the wrong attitude, taken the wrong path, said the wrong thing, or acted the wrong way. He is never too late or too early, too loud or too soft, too fast or too slow. He has always been and always will be right. He is righteous.

Traveling Light

They Couldn't Forget Him

"Jesus is the One whom God raised from the dead.
And we are all witnesses to this."

We don't know where the disciples went when they fled the garden, but we do know what they took: a memory. They took a heart-stopping memory of a man who called himself no less than God in the flesh. And they couldn't get him out of their minds. Try as they might to lose him in the crowd, they couldn't forget him.

If they saw a leper, they thought of his compassion.

If they heard a storm, they would remember the day he silenced one.

If they saw a child, they would think of the day he held one.

And if they saw a lamb being carried to the temple, they would remember his face streaked with blood and his eyes flooded with love.

No, they couldn't forget him. As a result, they came back. And, as a result, the church of our Lord began with a group of frightened men in an upper room.

Six Hours One Friday

The Proper View of Self

To him who is able to do exceedingly abundantly
above all that we ask or think . . . be glory.

EPHESIANS 3:20–21 NKJV

There are two extremes of poor I-sight.
Self-loving and self-loathing. We swing
from one side to the other. Promotions and
demotions bump us back and forth. One day too
high on self, the next too hard on self. Neither is
correct. Self-elevation and self-deprecation are
equally inaccurate. Where is the truth?

Smack-dab in the middle. Dead center
between "I can do anything" and "I can't do
anything" lies "I can do all things through Christ
who strengthens me" (Phil. 4:13).

Neither omnipotent nor impotent, neither
God's MVP nor God's mistake. Not self-secure or
insecure, but God-secure—a self-worth based in
our identity as children of God. The proper view
of self is in the middle.

Cure for the Common Life

A Robe of Righteousness

You were all clothed with Christ.

GALATIANS 3:27

We eat our share of forbidden fruit. We say what we shouldn't say. Go where we shouldn't go. Pluck fruit from trees we shouldn't touch.

And when we do, the door opens, and the shame tumbles in. And we hide. We sew fig leaves. . . . We cover ourselves in good works and good deeds, but one gust of the wind of truth, and we are naked again—stark naked in our own failure.

So what does God do? Exactly what he did for our parents in the garden. He sheds innocent blood. He offers the life of his Son. And from the scene of the sacrifice the Father takes a robe— the robe of righteousness. And does he throw it in our direction and tell us to shape up? No, he dresses us himself. He dresses us with himself. "You were all baptized into Christ, and so you were all clothed with Christ" (Gal. 3:26–27).

We hide. He seeks. We bring sin. He brings a sacrifice. We try fig leaves. He brings the robe of righteousness.

A Love Worth Giving

The Other Side of the River

I want to know Christ and the power that
raised him from the dead. . . . Then I have hope
that I myself will be raised from the dead.

PHILIPPIANS 3:10–11

Jesus saw people enslaved by their fear of death. He explained that the river of death was nothing to fear. The people wouldn't believe him. He touched a boy and called him back to life. The followers were still unconvinced. He whispered life into the dead body of a girl. The people were still cynical. He let a dead man spend four days in a grave and then called him out. Is that enough? Apparently not. For it was necessary for him to enter the river, to submerge himself in the water of death before people would believe that death had been conquered.

But after he did, after he came out on the other side of death's river, it was time to sing . . . it was time to celebrate.

Six Hours One Friday

Two Choices

"What should I do with Jesus, the one called the Christ?"

MATTHEW 27:22

Pilate is correct in his question. "What should I do with Jesus, the one called the Christ?"

Perhaps you, like Pilate, are curious about this one called Jesus.

What do you do with a man who claims to be God, yet hates religion? What do you do with a man who calls himself the Savior, yet condemns systems? What do you do with a man who knows the place and time of his death, yet goes there anyway? . . .

You have two choices.

You can reject him. That is an option. You can, as have many, decide that the idea of God's becoming a carpenter is too bizarre— and walk away.

Or you can accept him. You can journey with him. You can listen for his voice amid the hundreds of voices and follow him.

And the Angels Were Silent

Wrestling with God

"Your name will now be Israel, because you have wrestled with God and with people, and you have won."

The word *Jabbok* in Hebrew means "wrestle," and wrestle is what Jacob did. He wrestled with his past: all the white lies, scheming, and scandalizing. He wrestled with his situation: a spider trapped in his own web of deceit and craftiness. But more than anything, he wrestled with God. . . .

Jacob wrestled with God the entire night. On the banks of Jabbok he rolled in the mud of his mistakes. He met God face to face, sick of his past and in desperate need of a fresh start. And because Jacob wanted it so badly, God honored his determination. God gave him a new name and a new promise. But he also gave a wrenched hip as a reminder of that mysterious night at the river. . . .

We too should unmask our stained hearts and grimy souls and be honest with the One who knows our most secret sins.

The result could be refreshing. We know it was for Jacob. After his encounter with God, Jacob was a new man.

God Came Near

Perfect Love

Perfect love casts out fear.

1 JOHN 4:18 NKJV

Have you ever gone to the grocery on an empty stomach? You're a sitting duck. You buy everything you don't need. Doesn't matter if it is good for you—you just want to fill your tummy. When you're lonely, you do the same in life, pulling stuff off the shelf, not because you need it, but because you are hungry for love.

Why do we do it? Because we fear facing life alone. For fear of not fitting in, we take the drugs. For fear of standing out, we wear the clothes. For fear of appearing small, we go into debt and buy the house. For fear of going unnoticed, we dress to seduce or to impress. For fear of sleeping alone, we sleep with anyone. For fear of not being loved, we search for love in all the wrong places.

But all that changes when we discover God's perfect love. And "perfect love casts out fear."

Traveling Light

Watch and Pray

Watch and pray so that you will not fall into temptation.

MARK 14:38 NIV

"Watch." They don't come any more practical than that. Watch. Stay alert. Keep your eyes open. When you see sin coming, duck. When you anticipate an awkward encounter, turn around. When you sense temptation, go the other way.

All Jesus is saying is, "Pay attention." You know your weaknesses. You also know the situations in which your weaknesses are most vulnerable. Stay out of those situations. Back seats. Late hours. Movie theaters. Whatever it is that gives Satan a foothold in your life, stay away from it. Watch out!

"Pray." Prayer isn't telling God anything new. There is not a sinner nor a saint who would surprise him. What prayer does is invite God to walk the shadowy pathways of life with us. Prayer is asking God to watch ahead for falling trees and tumbling boulders and to bring up the rear, guarding our backside from the poison darts of the devil.

No Wonder They Call Him the Savior

What Will You Bring?

If we confess our sins, he will forgive our sins,
because we can trust God to do what is right.

1 JOHN 1:9

In order for the cross of Christ to be the cross of your life, you and I need to bring something to the hill.

We have seen what Jesus brought. With scarred hands he offered forgiveness. Through torn skin he promised acceptance. He took the path to take us home. He wore our garment to give us his own. We have seen the gifts he brought.

Now we ask, what will we bring? . . .

Why don't you start with your bad moments?

Those bad habits? Leave them at the cross. Your selfish moods and white lies? Give them to God. Your binges and bigotries? God wants them all. Every flop, every failure. He wants every single one. Why? Because he knows we can't live with them.

He Chose the Nails

Each Day Matters

*You were chosen to tell about the
excellent qualities of God.*

1 PETER 2:9 GOD'S WORD

Let's spend a lifetime making our heavenly
Father proud.

Use your uniqueness to do so. You exited the
womb called. Don't see yourself as a product of
your parents' DNA, but rather as a brand-new
idea from heaven.

Make a big deal out of God. Become who
you are for him! Has he not transferred you from
a dull, death-destined life to a rich, heaven-bound
adventure? Remember, "You were chosen to tell
about the excellent qualities of God." And do so
every day of your life.

With God, every day matters, every
person counts.

And that includes you.

Cure for the Common Life

Imitate Christ

Live a life of love, just as Christ loved us.

EPHESIANS 5:2 NIV

Long to be more loving? Begin by accepting your place as a dearly loved child. "Be imitators of God, therefore, as dearly loved children and live a life of love, just as Christ loved us" (Eph. 5:1–2 NIV).

Want to learn to forgive? Then consider how you've been forgiven. "Be kind and compassionate to one another, forgiving each other, just as in Christ God forgave you" (Eph. 4:32 NIV).

Finding it hard to put others first? Think of the way Christ put you first. "Though he was God, he did not demand and cling to his rights as God" (Phil. 2:6 NLT).

Need more patience? Drink from the patience of God (2 Pet. 3:9). Is generosity an elusive virtue? Then consider how generous God has been with you (Rom. 5:8). Having trouble putting up with ungrateful relatives or cranky neighbors? God puts up with you when you act the same. "He is kind to the ungrateful and wicked" (Luke 6:35 NIV).

A Love Worth Giving

June

Give all your worries to him,
because he cares about you.

—1 PETER 5:7

Jesus Honors You

It is good to . . . sing praises to Your name. . .
to declare Your lovingkindness in the morning.

PSALM 92 1–2 NKJV

Listen closely. Jesus' love does not depend
upon what we do for him. Not at all.
In the eyes of the King, you have value simply
because you are. You don't have to look nice or
perform well. Your value is inborn.

Period.

Think about that for just a minute. You are
valuable just because you exist. Not because of
what you do or what you have done, but simply
because you are. Remember that the next time
you are left bobbing in the wake of someone's
steamboat ambition. Remember that the next
time some trickster tries to hang a bargain
basement price tag on your self-worth. The next
time someone tries to pass you off as a cheap buy,
just think about the way Jesus honors you . . .
and smile.

I do. I smile because I know I don't deserve
love like that. None of us do.

No Wonder They Call Him the Savior

The Flagship of Patience

Love is patient.

1 CORINTHIANS 13:4

Paul presents patience as the premiere expression of love. Positioned at the head of the apostle's Love Armada—a boat-length or two in front of kindness, courtesy, and forgiveness—is the flagship known as patience. "Love is patient."

The Greek word used here for patience is a descriptive one. It figuratively means "taking a long time to boil." Think about a pot of boiling water. What factors determine the speed at which it boils? The size of the stove? No. The pot? The utensil may have an influence, but the primary factor is the intensity of the flame. Water boils quickly when the flame is high. It boils slowly when the flame is low. Patience "keeps the burner down."

Helpful clarification, don't you think? Patience isn't naive. It doesn't ignore misbehavior. It just keeps the flame low. It waits. It listens. It's slow to boil. This is how God treats us. And, according to Jesus, this is how we should treat others.

A Love Worth Giving

The Price of Self-Obsession

"I am the LORD. There is no other God."

ISAIAH 45:18

We pay a high price for . . . self-obsession. "God isn't pleased at being ignored" (Rom. 8:8 MSG). Paul speaks of sinners when he describes those who "knew God, but they wouldn't worship him as God. . . . So God let them go ahead and do whatever shameful things their hearts desired" (Rom. 1:21, 24 NASB).

You've seen the chaos. The husband ignoring his wife. The dictator murdering the millions. Grown men seducing the young. The young propositioning the old. When you do what you want, and I do what I want, and no one gives a lick as to what God wants, humanity implodes. The infection of the person leads to the corruption of the populace. . . .

Extract God; expect earthly chaos and, many times worse, expect eternal misery.

Come Thirsty

Our Servant Master

The Son of Man did not come to be served.
He came to serve others and
to give His life a ransom for many people.

MATTHEW 20:28

As a young boy, I read a Russian fable about a master and a servant who went on a journey to a city. Many of the details I've forgotten but the ending I remember. Before the two men could reach the destination they were caught in a blinding blizzard. They lost their direction and were unable to reach the city before nightfall.

The next morning concerned friends went searching for the two men. They finally found the master, frozen to death, face down in the snow. When they lifted him they found the servant— cold but alive. He survived and told how the master had voluntarily placed himself on top of the servant so the servant could live.

I hadn't thought of that story in years. But when I read what Christ said he would do for us, the story surfaced—for Jesus is the master who died for the servants.

And the Angels Were Silent

A Second Transformation

We shall all be changed—
in a moment, in the twinkling of an eye.

1 CORINTHIANS 15:51–52

"I am with you always" are the words of a God who in one instant did the impossible to make it all possible for you and me.(Matt. 28:20)

It all happened in a moment. In one moment . . . a most remarkable moment. The Word became flesh.

There will be another. The world will see another instantaneous transformation. You see, in becoming man, God made it possible for man to see God. When Jesus went home he left the back door open. As a result, "we shall all be changed— in a moment, in the twinkling of an eye."

The first moment of transformation went unnoticed by the world. But you can bet your sweet September that the second one won't.

God Came Near

Travel Light

Give all your worries to him, because he cares about you.

1 PETER 5:7

God has a great race for you to run. Under his care you will go where you've never been and serve in ways you've never dreamed. But you have to drop some stuff. How can you share grace if you are full of guilt? How can you offer comfort if you are disheartened? How can you lift someone else's load if your arms are full with your own?

For the sake of those you love, travel light.

For the sake of the God you serve, travel light.

For the sake of your own joy, travel light.

There are certain weights in life you simply cannot carry. Your Lord is asking you to set them down and trust him.

Traveling Light

What Love Does

*Christ Jesus . . . did not consider equality with
God something to be grasped, but made himself
nothing, taking the very nature of a servant.*

PHILIPPIANS 2:5–7 NIV

Would you do what Jesus did? He swapped
a spotless castle for a grimy stable. He
exchanged the worship of angels for the company
of killers. He could hold the universe in his palm
but gave it up to float in the womb of a maiden.

If you were God, would you sleep on straw,
nurse from a breast, and be clothed in a diaper?
I wouldn't, but Christ did.

If you knew that only a few would care that
you came, would you still come? If you knew
that those you loved would laugh in your face,
would you still care? . . . Christ did.

He humbled himself. He went from commanding
angels to sleeping in the straw. From holding stars
to clutching Mary's finger. The palm that held the
universe took the nail of a soldier.

Why? Because that's what love does. It puts
the beloved before itself.

A Love Worth Giving

Don't Give Up!

"It is finished."

JOHN 19:30

 Our inability to finish what we start is seen in the smallest of things:

A partly mowed lawn.

A half-read book.

Or, it shows up in life's most painful areas:

An abandoned child.

A wrecked marriage.

Any chance I'm addressing someone who is considering giving up? If I am, I want to encourage you to remain. I want to encourage you to remember Jesus' determination on the cross.

Jesus didn't quit. But don't think for one minute that he wasn't tempted to. Did he ever want to quit? You bet.

That's why his words are so splendid. "It is finished."

No Wonder They Call Him the Savior

Taking Inventory

*Don't you know that you are
God's temple and that God's Spirit lives in you?*

1 CORINTHIANS 3:18

All believers have God in their heart. But not all believers have given their whole heart to God. Remember, the question is not, how can I have more of the Spirit? but rather, how can the Spirit have more of me? Take inventory. As you look around your life, do you see any resistant pockets? . . . Go down the list. . . .

Your tongue. Do you tend to stretch the truth? Puff up the facts? Your language? Is your language a sewer of profanities and foul talk? And grudges? Do you keep resentments parked in your "garudge"? Are you unproductive and lazy? Do you live off the system, assuming that the church or the country should take care of you? . . .

Do your actions interrupt the flow of the Spirit in your life?

Come Thirsty

The Clothing on the Cross

He himself bore our sins in his body on the tree,
so that we might die to sins and live for righteousness.

1 PETER 2:24 NIV

When Christ was nailed to the cross, he took off his robe of seamless perfection and assumed a different wardrobe, the wardrobe of indignity.

The indignity of nakedness. Stripped before his own mother and loved ones. Shamed before his family.

The indignity of failure. For a few pain-filled hours, the religious leaders were the victors, and Christ appeared the loser. Shamed before his accusers.

Worst of all, he wore *the indignity of sin.* "He himself bore our sins in his body on the tree, so that we might die to sins and live for righteousness."

The clothing of Christ on the cross? Sin—yours and mine. The sins of all humanity.

He Chose the Nails

The God You Need

The LORD created the heavens. He is the God who formed the earth and made it.

ISAIAH 45:18

You don't need what Dorothy found. Remember her discovery in *The Wonderful Wizard of Oz?* She and her trio followed the yellow-brick road only to discover that the wizard was a wimp! Nothing but smoke and mirrors and tin-drum thunder. Is that the kind of god you need?

You don't need to carry the burden of a lesser god . . . a god on a shelf, a god in a box, or a god in a bottle. No, you need a God who can place 100 billion stars in our galaxy and 100 billion galaxies in the universe. You need a God who can shape two fists of flesh into 75 to 100 billion nerve cells, each with as many as 10,000 connections to other nerve cells, place it in a skull, and call it a brain.

And you need a God who, while so mind-numbingly mighty, can come in the soft of night and touch you with the tenderness of an April snow.

Traveling Light

The Big Choice Is Ours

"Come to me, . . . and I will give you rest."

MATTHEW 11:28

It is possible to learn much about God's invitation and never respond to it personally.

Yet his invitation is clear and nonnegotiable. He gives all and we give him all. Simple and absolute. He is clear in what he asks and clear in what he offers. The choice is up to us.

Isn't it incredible that God leaves the choice to us? Think about it. There are many things in life we can't choose. We can't, for example, choose the weather. We can't control the economy.

We can't choose whether or not we are born with a big nose or blue eyes or a lot of hair. We can't even choose how people respond to us.

But we can choose where we spend eternity. The big choice, God leaves to us. The critical decision is ours.

What are you doing with God's invitation?

And the Angels Were Silent

God Sees What We Can't

No one is like the LORD our God,
who rules from heaven.

PSALM 113:5

On a trip to the United Kingdom, our family visited a castle. In the center of the garden sat a maze. Row after row of shoulder-high hedges, leading to one dead end after another. Successfully navigate the labyrinth, and discover the door to a tall tower in the center of the garden. Were you to look at our family pictures of the trip, you'd see four of our five family members standing on the top of the tower. Hmmm, someone is still on the ground. Guess who? I was stuck in the foliage. I just couldn't figure out which way to go.

Ah, but then I heard a voice from above. "Hey, Dad." I looked up to see Sara, peering through the turret at the top. "You're going the wrong way," she explained. "Back up and turn right."

Do you think I trusted her? I didn't have to. But do you know what I did? I listened. Her vantage point was better than mine. She was above the maze. She could see what I couldn't.

Don't you think we should do the same with God?

Next Door Savior

He Doesn't Remember

"I will remember their sins no more."

HEBREWS 8:12 RSV

I was thanking the Father today for his mercy. I began listing the sins he'd forgiven. One by one I thanked God for forgiving my stumbles and tumbles. My motives were pure and my heart was thankful, but my understanding of God was wrong. It was when I used the word *remember* that it hit me.

"Remember the time I . . ." I was about to thank God for another act of mercy. But I stopped. Something was wrong. The word *remember* seemed displaced. . . . "Does he remember?"

Then *I* remembered. I remembered his words. "And I will remember their sins no more."

Wow! Now, *that* is a remarkable promise.

God doesn't just forgive, he forgets. . . . For all the things he does do, this is one thing he refuses to do. He refuses to keep a list of my wrongs.

God Came Near

A Personal Path

You, LORD, give perfect peace to those who keep their purpose firm and put their trust in you.

ISAIAH 26:3 TEV

When David volunteered to go mano a mano with Goliath, King Saul tried to clothe the shepherd boy with soldier's armor. After all, Goliath stood over nine feet tall. He wore a bronze helmet and a 125-pound coat of mail. He bore bronze leggings and carried a javelin and a spear with a 15-pound head (1 Sam. 17:4–7 NLT). And David? David had a slingshot. This is a VW Bug playing blink with an eighteen-wheeler. . . . When Saul saw David, pimpled, and Goliath, rippled, he did what any Iron Age king would do. "Saul gave David his own armor—a bronze helmet and a coat of mail" (1 Sam. 17:38 NLT). . . .

But David rejected the armor, selected the stones, lobotomized the giant, and taught us a powerful lesson: what fits others might not fit you. Indeed what fits *the king* might not fit you. Just because someone gives you advice, a job, or a promotion, you don't have to accept it. Let your uniqueness define your path of life.

Cure for the Common Life

The Intersection of Love

Though He was crucified in weakness,
yet He lives by the power of God.

2 CORINTHIANS 13:4 NKJV

The cross. Can you turn any direction without seeing one? Perched atop a chapel. Carved into a graveyard headstone. Engraved in a ring or suspended on a chain. The cross is the universal symbol of Christianity. An odd choice, don't you think? Strange that a tool of torture would come to embody a movement of hope. The symbols of other faiths are more upbeat: the six-pointed star of David, the crescent moon of Islam, a lotus blossom for Buddhism. Yet a cross for Christianity? An instrument of execution? . . .

Why is the cross the symbol of our faith? To find the answer look no farther than the cross itself. Its design couldn't be simpler. One beam horizontal—the other vertical. One reaches out—like God's love. The other reaches up—as does God's holiness. One represents the width of his love; the other reflects the height of his holiness. The cross is the intersection. The cross is where God forgave his children without lowering his standards.

He Chose the Nails

The Angels Offer Worship

All the angels stood around the throne . . .
saying: "Amen! Blessing and glory and wisdom . . .
be to our God forever and ever."

REVELATION 7:11–12 NKJV

Only one sight enthralls angels—God's face. They know that he is Lord of all.

And as a result, they worship him. Whether in the temple with Isaiah or the pasture with the Bethlehem shepherds, angels worship. . . .

"All the angels stood around the throne . . . saying: 'Amen! Blessing and glory and wisdom, thanksgiving and honor and power and might, be to our God forever and ever. Amen.'"

Doesn't their worship proclaim volumes about God's beauty? Angels could gaze at the Grand Tetons and Grand Canyon, Picasso paintings and the Sistine Chapel, but they choose, instead, to fix their eyes on the glory of God. They can't see enough of him, and they can't be silent about what they see.

Come Thirsty

Stubborn Love

"My son was dead, but now he is alive again!
He was lost, but now he is found!"

Jesus . . . summarized God's stubborn love with a parable. He told about a teenager who decided that life at the farm was too slow for his tastes. So with pockets full of inheritance money, he set out to find the big time. What he found instead were hangovers, fair-weather friends, and long unemployment lines. When he had had just about as much of the pig's life as he could take, he swallowed his pride, dug his hands deep into his empty pockets, and began the long walk home; all the while rehearsing a speech that he planned to give to his father.

He never used it. Just when he got to the top of the hill, his father, who'd been waiting at the gate, saw him. The boy's words of apology were quickly muffled by the father's words of forgiveness. . . .

If you ever wonder how God can use you to make a difference in your world, . . . look at the forgiveness found in those open arms and take courage.

No Wonder They Call Him the Savior

God Is Enough

Because your love is better than life,
my lips will glorify you. . . . My soul will be
satisfied as with the richest of foods.

PSALM 63:3, 5 NIV

When it comes to love: *Be careful.*

Before you walk down the aisle, take a good long look around. Make sure this is God's intended place for you. And, if you suspect it isn't, get out. Don't force what is wrong to be right. . . . Be careful.

And, until love is stirred, let God's love be enough for you. There are seasons when God allows us to feel the frailty of human love so we'll appreciate the strength of his love. Didn't he do this with David? Saul turned on him. Michal, his wife, betrayed him. Jonathan and Samuel were David's friends, but they couldn't follow him into the wilderness. Betrayal and circumstances left David alone. Alone with God. And, as David discovered, God was enough. David wrote these words in a desert: "Because your love is better than life, my lips will glorify you. . . . My soul will be satisfied as with the richest of foods."

A Love Worth Giving

The Path of Righteousness

He leads me in the paths of righteousness.

PSALM 23:3 NKJV

It was, at once, history's most beautiful and most horrible moment. Jesus stood in the tribunal of heaven. Sweeping a hand over all creation, he pleaded, "Punish me for their mistakes. See the murderer? Give me his penalty. The adulteress? I'll take her shame. The bigot, the liar, the thief? Do to me what you would do to them. Treat me as you would a sinner."

And God did. "For Christ died for sins once for all, the righteous for the unrighteous, to bring you to God" (1 Pet. 3:18 NIV). . . .

The path of righteousness is a narrow, winding trail up a steep hill. At the top of the hill is a cross. At the base of the cross are bags. Countless bags full of innumerable sins. Calvary is the compost pile for guilt. Would you like to leave yours there as well?

Traveling Light

The Savior Won

"God has made this Jesus,
whom you crucified, both Lord and Christ."

ACTS 2:36

A transformed group stood beside a transformed Peter as he announced: "Therefore let all Israel be assured of this: God has made this Jesus, whom you crucified, both Lord and Christ."

No timidity in his words. No reluctance. About three thousand people believed his message.

The apostles sparked a movement. The people became followers of the death-conqueror. They couldn't hear enough or say enough about him. People began to call them "Christ-ians." Christ was their model, their message. They preached "Jesus Christ and him crucified," not for the lack of another topic, but because they couldn't exhaust this one.

What unlocked the doors of the apostles' hearts?

Simple. They saw Jesus. They encountered the Christ. Their sins collided with their Savior and their Savior won!

Six Hours One Friday

Why Worship?

*With my mouth will I make known
Your faithfulness to all generations.*

PSALM 89:1 NKJV

During our summer vacation I took . . . advantage of the occasion to solicit a sailing lesson. Ever puzzled by the difference in leeward, starboard, and stern, I asked the crew a few questions. After a while the captain offered, "Would you like to sail us home?". . . He assured me I would have no trouble. "Target that cliff," he instructed. "Set your eyes and the boat on it."

I found the instruction hard to follow. Other sights invited my attention: the rich mahogany of the deck, rich foam cresting on the waves. I wanted to look at it all. But look too long and risk losing the course. The boat stayed on target as long as I set my eyes beyond the vessel.

Worship helps us do this in life. It lifts our eyes off the boat with its toys and passengers and sets them "on the realities of heaven, where Christ sits at God's right hand in the place of honor and power" (Col. 3:1 NLT).

Cure for the Common Life

What Love Does

*"I was without clothes,
and you gave me something to wear."*

MATTHEW 25:36

What if you were given the privilege of Mary? What if God himself were placed in your arms as a naked baby? Would you not do what she did? "She wrapped the baby with pieces of cloth" (Luke 2:7).

The baby Jesus, still wet from the womb, was cold and chilled. So this mother did what any mother would do; she did what love does: She covered him.

Wouldn't you cherish an opportunity to do the same? You have one. Such opportunities come your way every day. Jesus said, "I was without clothes, and you gave me something to wear. . . . I tell you the truth, anything you did for even the least of my people here, you also did for me" (Matt. 25:36, 40).

A Love Worth Giving

God's Surprises

*No one has ever imagined what
God has prepared for those who love him.*

1 CORINTHIANS 2:9

Have you got God figured out? Have you got God captured on a flowchart and frozen on a flannelboard? If so, then listen. Listen to God's surprises.

Hear the rocks meant for the body of the adulterous woman drop to the ground.

Listen as the Messiah whispers to the Samaritan woman, "I who speak to you am he."

Listen to the widow from Nain eating dinner with her son who is supposed to be dead. . . .

God appearing at the strangest of places. Doing the strangest of things. Stretching smiles where there had hung only frowns. Placing twinkles where there were only tears.

Six Hours One Friday

God In the Ordinary

In Christ we can come before
God with freedom and without fear.

EPHESIANS 3:12

God calls us in a real world. . . . He doesn't communicate by stacking stars in the heavens or reincarnating grandparents from the grave. . . .

He's not a magician or a good-luck charm or the man upstairs. He is, instead, the Creator of the universe who is right here in the thick of our day-to-day world who speaks to you more through cooing babies and hungry bellies than he ever will through horoscopes, zodiac papers, or weeping Madonnas.

If you get some supernatural vision or hear some strange voice in the night, don't get too carried away. It could be God or it could be indigestion, and you don't want to misinterpret one for the other.

God speaks in our world. We just have to learn to hear him . . . amidst the ordinary.

And the Angels Were Silent

One Explanation

After I rise from the dead,
I will go ahead of you into Galilee.

MATTHEW 26:32

Remember [Christ's] followers' fear at the crucifixion? They ran. Scared as cats in a dog pound. . . .

But fast-forward forty days. Bankrupt traitors have become a force of life-changing fury. Peter is preaching in the very precinct where Christ was arrested. Followers of Christ defy the enemies of Christ. Whip them and they'll worship. Lock them up and they'll launch a jailhouse ministry. As bold after the Resurrection as they were cowardly before it.

Explanation:

Greed? They made no money.

Power? They gave all the credit to Christ.

Popularity? Most were killed for their beliefs.

Only one explanation remains—a resurrected Christ and his Holy Spirit. The courage of these men and women was forged in the fire of the empty tomb.

Next Door Savior

When Hopes Don't Happen

In the time of trouble He shall hide me in His pavilion.

PSALM 27:5 NKJV

What do we do with our disappointments? We could do what Miss Haversham did. Remember her in Charles Dickens's *Great Expectations*? Jilted by her fiancé just prior to the wedding, . . . she closed all the blinds in the house, stopped every clock, left the wedding cake on the table to gather cobwebs, and wore her wedding dress until it hung in yellow decay around her shrunken form. Her wounded heart consumed her life.

We can follow the same course.

Or we can follow the example of the apostle Paul. His goal was to be a missionary in Spain, . . . however, God sent him to prison. Sitting in a Roman jail, Paul could have made the same choice as Miss Haversham, but he didn't. Instead he said, "As long as I'm here, I might as well write a few letters." Hence your Bible has the Epistles to Philemon, the Philippians, the Colossians, and the Ephesians.

Traveling Light

No Strings Attached

He is the One who loves us, who made us
free from our sins with the blood of his death.

When we love with expectations, we say,
"I love you. But I'll love you even more if . . ."
Christ's love had none of this. No strings,
no expectations, no hidden agendas, no secrets.
His love for us was, and is, up front and clear.
"I love you," he says. "Even if you let me down.
I love you in spite of your failures."

One step behind the expectations of Christ
come his forgiveness and tenderness. Tumble off
the tightrope of what our Master expects and you
land safely in his net of tolerance.

No Wonder They Call Him the Savior

Go First to God

> *"This is my commitment to*
> *my people: removal of their sins."*
>
> ROMANS 11:27 MSG

God does more than forgive our mistakes; he removes them! We simply have to take them to him.

He not only wants the mistakes we've made. He wants the ones we are making! Are you making some? Are you drinking too much? Are you cheating at work or cheating at marriage? Are you mismanaging money? Are you mismanaging your life?

If so, don't pretend nothing is wrong. Don't pretend you don't fall. Don't try to get back in the game. Go first to God. The first step after a stumble must be in the direction of the cross.

He Chose the Nails

Abounding Grace

*The more we see our sinfulness,
the more we see God's abounding grace.*

To abound is to have a surplus, an abundance, an extravagant portion. Should the fish in the Pacific worry that it will run out of ocean? No. Why? The ocean abounds with water. Need the lark be anxious about finding room in the sky to fly? No. The sky abounds with space.

Should the Christian worry that the cup of mercy will run empty? He may. For he may not be aware of God's abounding grace. Are you? Are you aware that the cup God gives you overflows with mercy? Or are you afraid your cup will run dry? Your warranty will expire? Are you afraid your mistakes are too great for God's grace? . . .

God is not a miser with his grace. Your cup may be low on cash or clout, but it is overflowing with mercy.

Traveling Light

July

*Guide me in your truth
and teach me, my God, my Savior.*

—Psalm 25:5

Spiritual Water

"The water I give will become a spring of water gushing up inside . . . giving eternal life."

JOHN 4:13

 Deprive your body of necessary fluid, and your body will tell you.

Deprive your soul of spiritual water, and your soul will tell you. Dehydrated hearts send desperate messages. Snarling tempers. Waves of worry. Growling mastodons of guilt and fear. You think God wants you to live with these? Hopelessness. Sleeplessness. Loneliness. Resentment. Irritability. Insecurity. These are warnings. Symptoms of a dryness deep within.

Treat your soul as you treat your thirst. Take a gulp. Imbibe moisture. Flood your heart with a good swallow of water.

Where do you find water for the soul? "If anyone thirsts, let him come to Me and drink."

Come Thirsty

The Time Line of History

He sent me to preach the Good news . . .
so that cross of Christ would not lose its power.

1 CORINTHIANS 1:17

The cross . . . rests on the time line of history like a compelling diamond. Its tragedy summons all sufferers. Its absurdity attracts all cynics. Its hope lures all searchers. . . .

History has idolized it and despised it, gold-plated it and burned it, worn and trashed it. History has done everything to it but ignore it.

That's the one option that the cross does not offer.

No one can ignore it! You can't ignore a piece of lumber that suspends the greatest claim in history. A crucified carpenter claiming that he is God on earth? Divine? Eternal? The death-slayer? . . .

To accept or reject Christ without a careful examination of Calvary is like deciding on a car without looking at the engine. Being religious without knowing the cross is like owning a Mercedes with no motor. Pretty package, but where is your power?

No Wonder They Call Him the Savior

A List of Our Sins

He canceled the record that contained the charges against us. He . . . destroyed it by nailing it to Christ's cross.

COLOSSIANS 2:14 NLT

Come with me to the hill of Calvary. . . . Watch as the soldiers shove the Carpenter to the ground and stretch his arms against the beams. One presses a knee against a forearm and a spike against a hand. Jesus turns his face toward the nail just as the soldier lifts the hammer to strike it.

The crowd at the cross concluded that the purpose of the pounding was to skewer the hands of Christ to a beam. But they were only half-right. We can't fault them for missing the other half. They couldn't see it. . . .

Between his hand and the wood there was a list. A long list. A list of our mistakes: our lusts and lies and greedy moments and prodigal years. A list of our sins.

The list, however, cannot be read. The words can't be deciphered. The mistakes are covered. The sins are hidden. Those at the top are hidden by his hand; those down the list are covered by his blood.

He Chose the Nails

Enough for Today

"I will cause food to fall like rain from the sky for all of you. Every day the people must go out and gather what they need for that day."

EXODUS 16:4

God liberated his children from slavery and created a path through the sea. He gave them a cloud to follow in the day and a fire to see at night. And he gave them food. He met their most basic need: He filled their bellies.

Each morning the manna came. Each evening the quail appeared. "Trust me. Trust me and I will give you what you need." The people were told to take just enough for one day. Their needs would be met, one day at a time.

"Just take enough for today," was God's message. "Let me worry about tomorrow."

The Father wanted the people to trust him.

And the Angels Were Silent

It's Inexplicable

The LORD who saves you is the Holy One of Israel.

ISAIAH 49:7

Even after generations of people had spit in his face, he still loved them. After a nation of chosen ones had stripped him naked and ripped his incarnated flesh, he still died for them. And even today, after billions have chosen to prostitute themselves before the pimps of power, fame, and wealth, he still waits for them.

It is inexplicable. It doesn't have a drop of logic nor a thread of rationality.

And yet, it is that very irrationality that gives the gospel its greatest defense. For only God could love like that. . . .

How absurd to think that such nobility would go to such poverty to share such a treasure with such thankless souls.

But he did.

God Came Near

Honest Evaluation

Guide me in your truth and teach me,
my God, my Savior.

PSALM 25:5

Raise your hand if any of the following describe you.

You are at peace with everyone. Every relationship as sweet as fudge. Even your old flames speak highly of you. Love all and are loved by all. Is that you?

You have no fears. Call you the Teflon toughie. Wall Street plummets—no problem. Heart condition discovered—yawn. Does this describe you?

You need no forgiveness. Never made a mistake. As square as a game of checkers. As clean as grandma's kitchen. Is that you? No?

Let's evaluate this. A few of your relationships are shaky. You have fears and faults. Hmmm. Do you really want to hang on to your chest of self-reliance? Sounds to me as if you could use a shepherd.

Traveling Light

Know Your Part

Consider others better than yourselves.

PHILIPPIANS 2:3 NIV

True humility is not thinking lowly of yourself but thinking accurately of yourself. The humble heart does not say, "I can't do anything." But rather, "I can't do everything. I know my part and am happy to do it."

When Paul writes "*consider* others better than yourselves" (Phil. 2:3 NIV, emphasis mine), he uses a verb that means "to calculate," "to reckon." The word implies a conscious judgment resting on carefully weighed facts. To consider others better than yourself, then, is not to say you have no place; it is to say that you know your place. "Don't cherish exaggerated ideas of yourself or your importance, but try to have a sane estimate of your capabilities by the light of the faith that God has given to you" (Rom. 12:3 PHILLIPS).

A Love Worth Giving

Endure to the End

*Those people who keep their faith
until the end will be saved.*

MATTHEW 10:22

Are you close to quitting? Please don't do it.
Are you discouraged as a parent? Hang in
there. Are you weary with doing good? Do just a
little more. Are you pessimistic about your job?
Roll up your sleeves and go at it again. No
communication in your marriage? Give it one
more shot. . . .

Remember, a finisher is not one with no
wounds or weariness. Quite to the contrary, he,
like the boxer, is scarred and bloody. Mother
Teresa is credited with saying, "God didn't call us
to be successful, just faithful." The fighter, like our
Master, is pierced and full of pain. He, like Paul,
may even be bound and beaten. But he remains.

The Land of Promise, says Jesus, awaits those
who endure. It is not just for those who make the
victory laps or drink champagne. No sir. The
Land of Promise is for those who simply remain
to the end.

No Wonder They Call Him the Savior

Christ Came to Serve

They all may call on the name of the LORD,
to serve Him with one accord.

ZEPHANIAH 33:9 NKJV

Jesus came to serve.

He let a woman in Samaria interrupt his rest, a woman in adultery interrupt his sermon, a woman with a disease interrupt his plans, and one with remorse interrupt his meal.

Though none of the apostles washed his feet, he washed theirs. Though none of the soldiers at the cross begged for mercy, he extended it. And though his followers skedaddled like scared rabbits on Thursday, he came searching for them on Easter Sunday. The resurrected King ascended to heaven only after he'd spent forty days with his friends—teaching them, encouraging them . . . serving them.

Why? It's what he came to do. He came to serve.

Cure for the Common Life

Sealed with the Spirit

Having believed, you were marked in him
with a seal, the promised Holy Spirit.

EPHESIANS 1:13 NIV

The most famous New Testament
"sealing" occurred with the tomb of Jesus.
Roman soldiers rolled a rock over the entrance
and "set a seal on the stone" (Matt. 27:66 NASB).
Archaeologists envision two ribbons stretched in
front of the entrance, glued together with
hardened wax that bore the imprimatur of the
Roman government—SPQR *(Senatus Populusque
Romanus)*—as if to say, "Stay away! The contents
of this tomb belong to Rome." Their seal, of
course, proved futile.

The seal of the Spirit, however, proves
forceful. When you accepted Christ, God sealed
you with the Spirit. "Having believed, you were
marked in him with a seal, the promised Holy
Spirit." When hell's interlopers come seeking to
snatch you from God, the seal turns them away.
He bought you, owns you, and protects you. God
paid too high a price to leave you unguarded.

Come Thirsty

The Via Dolorosa

God was in Christ reconciling the world to Himself.

2 CORINTHIANS 5:19 NKJV

The most notorious road in the world is the Via Dolorosa, "the Way of Sorrows." According to tradition, it is the route Jesus took from Pilate's hall to Calvary. The path is marked by stations frequently used by Christians for their devotions. One station marks the passing of Pilate's verdict. Another, the appearance of Simon to carry the cross. There are fourteen stations in all, each one a reminder of the events of Christ's final journey.

Is the route accurate? Probably not. . . . No one knows the exact route Christ followed that Friday.

But we do know where the path actually began.

The path began, not in the court of Pilate, but in the halls of heaven. The Father began his journey when he left his home in search of us. . . . His desire was singular—to bring his children home. . . .

The path to the cross tells us exactly how far God will go to call us back.

He Chose the Nails

People Who Make a Difference

Good people have good things in their hearts.

MATTHEW 12:35

Name the ten wealthiest men in the world.
Name eight people who have won the
Nobel or Pulitzer prize.

How did you do? I didn't do well either.
With the exception of you trivia hounds, none of
us remember the headliners of yesterday too well.
Surprising how quickly we forget, isn't it? And
what I've mentioned above are no second-rate
achievements. These are the best in their fields.
But the applause dies. Awards tarnish. Achievements
are forgotten.

Here's another quiz. See how you do on
this one.

Name ten people who have taught you
something worthwhile.

Name five friends who have helped you in a
difficult time.

Easier? It was for me, too. The lesson? The
people who make a difference are not the ones with
the credentials, but the ones with the concern.

And the Angels Were Silent

The Present-Tense Christ

Jesus Christ is the same yesterday, today, and forever.

HEBREWS 13:8

 "I am God's Son" (John 10:36 NCV).

"I am the resurrection and the life" (John 11:25).

"I am the way, and the truth, and the life" (John 14:6).

"I am the true vine" (John 15:1).

The present-tense Christ. He never says, "I was." We do. We do because "we were." We were younger, faster, prettier. Prone to be people of the past tense, we reminisce. Not God. Unwavering in strength, he need never say, "I was."

From the center of the storm, the unwavering Jesus shouts, "I am." Tall in the Trade Tower wreckage. Bold against the Galilean waves. ICU, battlefield, boardroom, prison cell, or maternity ward—whatever your storm, "I am."

Next Door Savior

God Forgets

Bless the LORD, . . . who forgives all your iniquities.

PSALM 103:1–2 NKJV

God doesn't remember the past. But I do, you do. You still remember. You're like me. You still remember what you did before you changed. In the cellar of your heart lurk the ghosts of yesterday's sins. Sins you've confessed; errors of which you've repented; damage you've done your best to repair. . . .

That horrid lie.

The time you exploded in anger.

Now, honestly. Do you think God was exaggerating when he said he would cast our sins as far as the east is from the west? Do you actually believe he would make a statement like "I will not hold their iniquities against them" and then rub our noses in them whenever we ask for help?

Of course you don't. You and I just need an occasional reminder of God's nature, his forgetful nature.

God Came Near

Guard Against Greed

Whoever loves money never has money enough;
whoever loves wealth is never satisfied with his income.

ECCLESIASTES 5:10 NIV

Greed comes in many forms. Greed for approval. Greed for applause. Greed for status. Greed for the best office, the fastest car, the prettiest date. Greed has many faces, but speaks one language: the language of more. Epicurus noted, "Nothing is enough for the man to whom enough is too little." And what was that observation of John D. Rockefeller's? He was asked, "How much money does it take to satisfy a man?" He answered, "Just a little more." Wise was the one who wrote, "Whoever loves money never has money enough; whoever loves wealth is never satisfied with his income" (Eccles. 5:10 NIV).

Greed has a growling stomach. Feed it, and you risk more than budget-busting debt. You risk losing purpose.

Cure for the Common Life

No Limit to His Love

This is how we know what real love is:
Jesus gave his life for us.

1 JOHN 3:16

It's nice to be included. You aren't always. Universities exclude you if you aren't smart enough. Businesses exclude you if you aren't qualified enough, and, sadly, some churches exclude you if you aren't good enough.

But though they may exclude you, Christ includes you. When asked to describe the width of his love, he stretched one hand to the right and the other to the left and had them nailed in that position so you would know he died loving you.

But isn't there a limit? Surely there has to be an end to this love. You'd think so, wouldn't you? But David the adulterer never found it. Paul the murderer never found it. Peter the liar never found it. When it came to life, they hit bottom. But when it came to God's love, they never did.

He Chose the Nails

God, Your Guardian

He will cover you with his feathers, and
under his wings you can hide.

PSALM 91:4

The image of living beneath *Shaddai's* shadow reminds me of a rained-out picnic. My college friends and I barely escaped a West Texas storm before it pummeled the park where we were spending a Saturday afternoon. As we were leaving, my buddy brought the car to a sudden stop and gestured to a tender sight on the ground. A mother bird sat exposed to the rain, her wing extended over her baby who had fallen out of the nest. The fierce storm prohibited her from returning to the tree, so she covered her child until the wind passed.

From how many winds is God protecting you? His wing, at this moment, shields you. A slanderous critic heading toward your desk is interrupted by a phone call. A burglar en route to your house has a flat tire. A drunk driver runs out of gas before your car passes his. God, your guardian, protects you.

Come Thirsty

Contentment

*He who follows righteousness and
mercy finds life, righteousness and honor.*

PROVERBS 21:21 NKJV

In our world, contentment is a strange
street vendor, roaming, looking for a home,
but seldom finding an open door. He moves
slowly from house to house, knocking on doors,
offering his wares: an hour of peace, a smile of
acceptance, a sigh of relief. But his goods are
seldom taken. We are too busy to be content.

"Not now, thank you. I've too much to do,"
we say. "Too many marks to be made, too many
achievements to be achieved. . . ."

So the vendor moves on. When I asked him
why so few welcomed him into their homes, his
answer left me convicted. "I charge a high price,
you know. My fee is steep. I ask people to trade in
their schedules, frustrations, and anxieties. I demand
that they put a torch to their fourteen-hour days
and sleepless nights. You'd think I'd have more
buyers." He scratched his beard, then added
pensively, "But people seem strangely proud of
their ulcers and headaches."

No Wonder They Call Him the Savior

You Make the Choice

Be careful what you think,
because your thoughts run your life.

PROVERBS 4:23

You are driving to work when the words of your coworker come to mind. He needled you about your performance. He second-guessed your efficiency. Why was he so hard on you? You begin to wonder. *I didn't deserve any of that. Who is he to criticize me? Besides, he has as much taste as a rice cake. Have you seen those shoes he wears?*

At this point you need to make a choice. *Am I going to keep a list of these wrongs?* You can. . . .

Or you can do something else. You can take those thoughts captive. You can defy the culprit. Quote a verse if you have to: "Bless those who persecute you; bless and do not curse" (Rom. 12:14 NIV). . . .

You are not a victim of your thoughts. You have a vote. You have a voice.

A Love Worth Giving

God Loves Humility

He crowns the humble with salvation.

PSALM 149:4 NIV

With the same intensity that he hates arrogance, God loves humility. The Jesus who said, "I am gentle and humble in heart" (Matt. 11:29 NASB) loves those who are gentle and humble in heart. "Though the LORD is supreme, he takes care of those who are humble" (Ps. 138:6). God says, "I live with people who are . . . humble" (Isa. 57:15). He also says, "To this one I will look, to him who is humble and contrite" (Isa. 66:2 NASB). And to the humble, God gives great treasures:

He gives honor: "Humility goes before honor" (Prov. 15:33 NRSV).

He gives wisdom: "With the humble is wisdom" (Prov. 11:2 NASB).

He gives direction: "He teaches the humble His way" (Ps. 25:9 NASB).

And most significantly, he gives grace: "God . . . gives grace to the humble" (1 Pet. 5:5).

Traveling Light

Our Loving Father

*The Father has loved us so much
that we are called children of God.*

1 JOHN 3:1

When my oldest daughter, Jenna, was four
years old, she came to me with a confession.
"Daddy, I took a crayon and drew on the wall."
(Kids amaze me with their honesty.)

I sat down and lifted her up into my lap and
tried to be wise. "Is that a good thing to do?"
I asked her.

"No."

"What does Daddy do when you write on
the wall?"

"You spank me."

"What do you think Daddy should do
this time?"

"Love."

Don't we all want that? Don't we all long for
a father who, even though our mistakes are
written all over the wall, will love us anyway?

We do have that type of a father. A father
who is at his best when we are at our worst.
A father whose grace is strongest when our
devotion is weakest.

Six Hours One Friday

What Worship Does

You who fear the LORD, praise Him!

PSALM 22:23 NKJV

Worship humbles the smug and lifts the deflated.

Worship adjusts us, lowering the chin of the haughty, straightening the back of the burdened.

Worship properly positions the worshiper. And oh how we need it! We walk through life so bent out of shape. Five-talent folks swaggering: "I bet God's glad to have me." Two-talent folks struggling: "I bet God's sick of putting up with me." So sold on ourselves that we think someone died and made us ruler. Or so down on ourselves that we think everyone died and just left us.

Treat both conditions with worship.

Cure for the Common Life

Just Be There

*The person who shows mercy can
stand without fear at the judgment.*

JAMES 2:13

Nothing takes the place of your presence.
Letters are nice. Phone calls are special, but
being there in the flesh sends a message.

After Albert Einstein's wife died, his sister,
Maja, moved in to assist with the household
affairs. For fourteen years she cared for him,
allowing his valuable research to continue. In 1950
she suffered a stroke and lapsed into a coma.
Thereafter, Einstein spent two hours every afternoon
reading aloud to her from Plato. She gave no sign
of understanding his words, but he read anyway.
If she understood anything by his gesture, she
understood this—he believed that she was worth
his time.

Do you believe in your kids? Then show up.
Show up at their games. Show up at their plays. . . .
Do you believe in your friends? Then show up.
Show up at their graduations and weddings.
Spend time with them. You want to bring out the
best in someone? Then show up.

A Love Worth Giving

Failures Are Not Fatal

We must pay more careful attention . . .
to what we have heard, so that we do not drift away.

HEBREWS 2:1 NIV

If you lose your faith, you will probably do so gradually. You will let a few days slip by without consulting your compass. Your sails will go untrimmed. Your rigging will go unprepared. And worst of all, you will forget to anchor your boat. And, before you know it, you'll be bouncing from wave to wave in stormy seas.

And unless you anchor deep, you could go down.

How do you anchor deep? Look at the verse again: "We must pay more careful attention . . . *to what we have heard. . . .*"

The most reliable anchor points are not recent discoveries, but are time-tested truths that have held their ground against the winds of change. Truths like: My life is not futile.

My failures are not fatal.

My death is not final.

Attach your soul to these boulders and no wave is big enough to wash you under.

Six Hours One Friday

More than Family

Each of us finds our meaning and
function as a part of his body.

ROMANS 12:5 MSG

 If similar experiences create friendships,
shouldn't the church overflow with
friendships? With whom do you have more in
common than fellow believers? Amazed by the
same manger, stirred by the same Bible, saved by
the same cross, and destined for the same home.
Can you not echo the words of the psalmist?
"I am a friend to everyone who fears you, to
anyone who obeys your orders" (Ps. 119:63).

The church. More than family, we are
friends. More than friends, we are family. God's
family of friends.

Cure for the Common Life

God Created All Things

*By Him all things were created, both in the heavens
and on earth, visible and invisible, whether thrones or
dominions or rulers or authorities—all things have
been created through Him and for Him.*

COLOSSIANS 1:16 NASB

What a phenomenal list! Heavens and earth. Visible and invisible. Thrones, dominions, rulers, and authorities. No thing, place, or person omitted. The scale on the sea urchin. The hair on the elephant hide. The hurricane that wrecks the coast, the rain that nourishes the desert, the infant's first heartbeat, the elderly person's final breath— all can be traced back to the hand of Christ, the firstborn of creation.

Firstborn in Paul's vernacular has nothing to do with birth order. Firstborn refers to order of rank. As one translation states: "He ranks higher than everything that has been made" (v.15 NCV). Everything? Find an exception. Peter's mother-in-law has a fever; Jesus rebukes it. A tax needs to be paid; Jesus pays it by sending first a coin and then a fisherman's hook into the mouth of a fish. Jesus . . . bats an eyelash, and nature jumps.

Next Door Savior

Bow Before Him

*God will always give what is right
to his people who cry to him night and day.*

LUKE 18:7

Jesus tends to his sheep. And he will tend
to you.

If you will let him. How? How do you let
him? The steps are so simple.

First, go to him. David would trust his wounds
to no other person but God. He said, "*You* anoint
my head with oil" (Ps. 23:5 NKJV). Not, "your
prophets," "your teachers," or "your counselors."

Your second step is to assume the right posture.
Bow before God.

In order to be anointed, the sheep must stand
still, lower their heads, and let the shepherd do his
work. Peter urges us to "be humble under God's
powerful hand so he will lift you up when the
right time comes" (1 Pet. 5:6).

When we come to God, we make requests;
we don't make demands. We come with high hopes
and a humble heart. We state what we want, but
we pray for what is right.

We go to him. We bow before him, and we
trust in him.

Traveling Light

Consistent Inconsistencies

*Strengthen yourselves so that you will
live here on earth doing what God wants.*

1 PETER 4:2

I suspect the most consistent thing about
life has to be its inconsistency. . . .

It's this eerie inconsistency that keeps all of
us, to one degree or another, living our lives on
the edge of our chairs.

Yet, it was in this inconsistency that God had
his finest hour. Never did the obscene come so
close to the holy as it did on Calvary. Never did
the good in the world so intertwine with the bad
as it did on the cross. . . .

God on a cross. Humanity at its worst.
Divinity at its best. . . .

God is not stumped by an evil world. He
doesn't gasp in amazement at the depth of our
faith or the depth of our failures. He knows the
condition of the world . . . and loves it just the
same. For just when we find a place where God
would never be (like on a cross), we look again
and there he is, in the flesh.

No Wonder They Call Him the Savior

God Wants Your List

Love does not keep a record of wrongs.

1 Corinthians 13:5 tev

Do you remember the story about the man who was bitten by the dog? When he learned the dog had rabies, he began making a list. The doctor told him there was no need to make a will, that rabies could be cured. "Oh, I'm not making a will," he replied. "I'm making a list of all the people I want to bite."

Couldn't we all make such a list? You've already learned, haven't you, that friends aren't always friendly? Neighbors aren't always neighborly? Some workers never work, and some bosses are always bossy?

You've already learned, haven't you, that a promise made is not always a promise kept? Even though they said "yes" on the altar, they may say "no" in the marriage.

You've already learned, haven't you, that we tend to fight back? To keep lists and snarl lips and growl at people we don't like?

God wants your list. He wants you to leave the list at the cross.

He Chose the Nails

Bending Low

Every knee will bow to the name of Jesus.

PHILIPPIANS 2:9–10

Servants resist stubbornness. Ulrich Zwingli manifested such a spirit. He promoted unity during Europe's great Reformation. At one point he found himself at odds with Martin Luther. Zwingli did not know what to do. He found his answer one morning on the side of a Swiss mountain. He watched two goats traversing a narrow path from opposite directions, one ascending, the other descending. At one point the narrow trail prevented them from passing each other. When they saw each other, they backed up and lowered their heads, as though ready to lunge. But then a wonderful thing happened. The ascending goat lay down on the path. The other stepped over his back. The first animal then arose and continued his climb to the top. Zwingli observed that the goat made it higher because he was willing to bend lower.

Didn't the same happen to Jesus? "God made his name greater than every other name so that every knee will bow to the name of Jesus."

Cure for the Common Life

God Gives Hope

God will help you overflow with hope in him
through the Holy Spirit's power within you.

ROMANS 15:13 TLB

Heaven's hope does for your world what
the sunlight did for my grandmother's
cellar. I owe my love of peach preserves to her.
She canned her own and stored them in an
underground cellar near her West Texas house.
It was a deep hole with wooden steps, plywood
walls, and a musty smell. As a youngster I used to
climb in, close the door, and see how long I could
last in the darkness. . . . I would sit silently,
listening to my breath and heartbeats, until I
couldn't take it anymore and then would race up
the stairs and throw open the door. Light would
avalanche into the cellar. What a change!
Moments before I couldn't see anything—all of a
sudden I could see everything.

Just as light poured into the cellar, God's
hope pours into your world. Upon the sick, he
shines the ray of healing. To the bereaved, he gives
the promise of reunion. To the confused, he offers
the light of Scripture.

Traveling Light

August

Life is not defined by what you have,
even when you have a lot.

—LUKE 12:15 MSG

He Did It for You

*All things are worth nothing compared
with the greatness of knowing Christ Jesus my Lord.*

PHILIPPIANS 3:8

Want to know the coolest thing about
Christ's coming?

Not that the One who hung the galaxies gave
it up to hang doorjambs to the displeasure of a
cranky client who wanted everything yesterday
but couldn't pay for anything until tomorrow.

Not that he refused to defend himself when
blamed for every sin of every slut and sailor since
Adam. . . .

Not even that after three days in a dark hole
he stepped into the Easter sunrise with a smile
and a swagger and a question for lowly Lucifer—
"Is that your best punch?"

That was cool, incredibly cool.

But want to know the coolest thing about the
One who gave up the crown of heaven for a
crown of thorns? He did it for you. Just for you.

He Chose the Nails

God's Bottomless Well

*"If anyone believes in me, rivers of living water
will flow out from that person's heart."*

Don't you need regular sips from God's
reservoir? I do. In countless situations—
stressful meetings, dull days, long drives,
demanding trips—and many times a day, I step to
the underground spring of God. There I receive
anew his work for my sin and death, the energy of
his Spirit, his lordship, and his love.

Drink with me from his bottomless **well**.
You don't have to live with a dehydrated heart.

Receive Christ's ***work*** on the cross,
the **e**nergy of his Spirit,
his ***lordship*** over your life,
his unending, unfailing ***love***.

Drink deeply and often. And out of you will
flow rivers of living water.

Come Thirsty

Some Days Never Come

If we love each other, God lives in us,
and his love is made perfect in us.

1 JOHN 4:12

Someday. The enemy of risky love is a snake whose tongue has mastered the talk of deception. "Someday," he hisses.

"Someday, I can take her on the cruise."

"Someday, I will have time to call and chat."

"Someday, the children will understand why I was so busy."

But you know the truth, don't you? You know even before I write it. You could say it better than I.

Some days never come. And the price of practicality is sometimes higher than extravagance. But the rewards of risky love are always greater than its cost.

Go to the effort. Invest the time. Write the letter. Make the apology. Take the trip. Purchase the gift. Do it. The seized opportunity renders joy. The neglected brings regret.

And the Angels Were Silent

Majestic Message

*"You will name him Jesus,
because he will save his people from their sins."*

MATTHEW 1:21

Many of the names in the Bible that refer to our Lord are nothing less than palatial and august: Son of God, The Lamb of God, The Light of the World, The Resurrection and the Life, The Bright and Morning Star, He that Should Come, Alpha and Omega.

They are phrases that stretch the boundaries of human language in an effort to capture the uncapturable, the grandeur of God. And try as they might to draw as near as they may, they always fall short. Hearing them is somewhat like hearing a Salvation Army Christmas band on the street corner play Handel's *Messiah*. Good try, but it doesn't work. The message is too majestic for the medium.

And such it is with language. The phrase "There are no words to express . . ." is really the only one that can honestly be applied to God. No names do him justice.

God Came Near

The Prison of Want

*Life is not defined by what you have,
even when you have a lot.*

LUKE 12:15 MSG

Are you in prison? You are if you feel better when you have more and worse when you have less. You are if joy is one delivery away, one transfer away, one award away, or one makeover away. If your happiness comes from something you deposit, drive, drink, or digest, then face it—you are in prison, the prison of want.

That's the bad news. The good news is, you have a visitor. And your visitor has a message that can get you paroled. Make your way to the receiving room. Take your seat in the chair, and look across the table at the psalmist David. He motions for you to lean forward. "I have a secret to tell you," he whispers, "the secret of satisfaction. 'The Lord is my shepherd; I shall not want'" (Ps. 23:1 NKJV).

It's as if he is saying, "What I have in God is greater than what I don't have in life."

You think you and I could learn to say the same?

Traveling Light

Love Doesn't Boast

Love does not boast, it is not proud.

1 CORINTHIANS 13:4 NIV

The humble heart honors others.

Is Jesus not our example? Content to be known as a carpenter. Happy to be mistaken for the gardener. He served his followers by washing their feet. He serves us by doing the same. Each morning he gifts us with beauty. Each Sunday he calls us to his table. Each moment he dwells in our hearts. And does he not speak of the day when he as "the master will dress himself to serve and tell the servants to sit at the table, and he will serve them" (Luke 12:37)?

If Jesus is so willing to honor us, can we not do the same for others? Make people a priority. Accept your part in his plan. Be quick to share the applause. And, most of all, regard others as more important than yourself. Love does. For love "does not boast, it is not proud."

A Love Worth Giving

An Undeserved Gift

Many people received God's gift of life by the grace of the one man, Jesus Christ.

ROMANS 5:15

We take our free gift of salvation and try to earn it or diagnose it or pay for it instead of simply saying "thank you" and accepting it.

Ironic as it may appear, one of the hardest things to do is to be saved by grace. There's something in us that reacts to God's free gift. We have some weird compulsion to create laws, systems, and regulations that will make us "worthy" of our gift.

Why do we do that? The only reason I can figure is pride. To accept grace means to accept its necessity, and most folks don't like to do that. To accept grace also means that one realizes his despair, and most people aren't too keen on doing that either.

No Wonder They Call Him the Savior

You Belong to Him

The love of God has been poured out in our hearts by the Holy Spirit.

ROMANS 5:5 NKJV

Deep within you, God's Spirit confirms with your spirit that you belong to him. Beneath the vitals of the heart, God's Spirit whispers, "You are mine. I bought you and sealed you, and no one can take you." The Spirit offers an inward, comforting witness.

He is like a father who walks hand in hand with his little child. The child knows he belongs to his daddy, his small hand happily lost in the large one. He feels no uncertainty about his papa's love. But suddenly the father, moved by some impulse, swings his boy up into the air and into his arms and says, "I love you, Son." . . .

Has the relationship between the two changed? On one level, no. The father is no more the father than he was before the expression of love. But on a deeper level, yes. The dad drenched, showered, and saturated the boy in love. God's Spirit does the same with us. . . . The Holy Spirit pours the love of God in our hearts.

Come Thirsty

He Took Our Place

*Christ . . . changed places with us and
put himself under that curse.*

GALATIANS 3:13

While on the cross, Jesus felt the indignity
and disgrace of a criminal. No, he was not
guilty. No, he had not committed a sin. And, no,
he did not deserve to be sentenced. But you and I
were, we had, and we did. We were left with nothing
to offer but a prayer. . . .

"He changed places with us." He wore our
sin so we could wear his righteousness.

Though we come to the cross dressed in sin,
we leave the cross dressed in the "coat of his
strong love" (Isa. 59:17) and girded with a belt of
"goodness and fairness" (Isa. 11:5) and clothed in
"garments of salvation" (Isa. 61:10 NIV).

Indeed, we leave dressed in Christ himself.
"You have all put on Christ as a garment"
(Gal. 3:27 NEB).

He Chose the Nails

It Defies Logic

"Here is my servant whom I have chosen. I love him,
and I am pleased with him."

Those who saw Jesus—really saw him—
knew there was something different. At his
touch blind beggars saw. At his command crippled
legs walked. At his embrace empty lives filled
with vision.

He fed thousands with one basket. He stilled
a storm with one command. He raised the dead
with one proclamation. He changed lives with
one request. He rerouted the history of the world
with one life, lived in one country, was born in
one manger, and died on one hill. . . .

God did what we wouldn't dare dream.
He did what we couldn't imagine. He became a
man so we could trust him. He became a sacrifice
so we could know him. And he defeated death so
we could follow him.

It defies logic. It is a divine insanity. A holy
incredibility.

Only a Creator beyond the fence of logic
could offer such a gift of love.

And the Angels Were Silent

You Have to Choose

I am the way, and the truth, and
the truth, and the way to the Father is through me.

JOHN 14:6

The definitive voice in the universe is
Jesus. . . .

He leaves us with two options. Accept him as
God, or reject him. . . . There is no third alternative.

Oh, but we try to create one. Suppose I did
the same? Suppose you came across me standing
on the side of the road. I can go north or south.
You ask me which way I'm going. My reply?
"I'm going sorth."

Thinking you didn't hear correctly, you ask
me to repeat the answer.

"I'm going sorth. I can't choose between north
and south, so I'm going both. I'm going sorth."

"You can't do that," you reply. "You have
to choose."

"OK," I concede, "I'll head nouth."

"Nouth is not an option!" you insist.
"It's either north or south. You gotta pick."

When it comes to Christ, you've got to do
the same.

Next Door Savior

Loving Forgetfulness

"I will forgive their iniquity,
and their sin I will remember no more."

JEREMIAH 31:34 NKJV

To love conditionally is against God's nature. Just as it's against your nature to eat trees and against mine to grow wings, it's against God's nature to remember forgiven sins.

You see, God is either the God of perfect grace . . . or he is not God. Grace forgets. Period. He who is perfect love cannot hold grudges. If he does, then he isn't perfect love. And if he isn't perfect love, you might as well put this book down and go fishing, because both of us are chasing fairy tales.

But I believe in his loving forgetfulness. And I believe he has a graciously terrible memory.

God Came Near

Choosing to Be Content

I have learned in whatever state I am, to be content.

PHILIPPIANS 4:11 NKJV

In his book *Money: A User's Manual,* Bob Russell describes a farmer who once grew discontent with his farm. He griped about the lake on his property always needing to be stocked and managed. . . . And those fat cows lumbered through his pasture. All the fencing and feeding—what a headache! . . .

He called a Realtor and made plans to list the farm. A few days later the agent phoned, wanting approval for the advertisement she intended to place in the local paper. She read the ad to the farmer. It described a lovely farm in an ideal location—quiet and peaceful, contoured with rolling hills, carpeted with soft meadows, nourished by a fresh lake, and blessed with well-bred livestock. The farmer said, "Read that ad to me again."

After hearing it a second time, he decided, "I've changed my mind. I'm not going to sell. I've been looking for a place like that all my life."

Cure for the Common Life

A Real Friend

A real friend will be more loyal than a brother.

PROVERBS 18:24

To others, Jesus was a miracle worker. To others, Jesus was a master teacher. To others, Jesus was the hope of Israel. But to John, he was all of these and more. To John, Jesus was a friend.

You don't abandon a friend—not even when that friend is dead. John stayed close to Jesus.

He had a habit of doing this. He was close to Jesus in the upper room. He was close to Jesus in the Garden of Gethsemane. He was at the foot of the cross at the crucifixion, and he was a quick walk from the tomb at the burial.

Did he understand Jesus? No.

Was he glad Jesus did what he did? No.

But did he leave Jesus? No.

What about you?

He Chose the Nails

Headed Home

We are waiting for God to finish making us his own children, which means our bodies will be made free.

ROMANS 8:23

Aging is God's idea. It's one of the ways he keeps us headed homeward. We can't change the process, but we can change our attitude. Here is a thought. What if we looked at the aging body as we look at the growth of a tulip?

Do you ever see anyone mourning over the passing of the tulip bulb? Do gardeners weep as the bulb begins to weaken? Of course not. We don't purchase tulip girdles or petal wrinkle cream or consult plastic-leaf surgeons. We don't mourn the passing of the bulb; we celebrate it. Tulip lovers rejoice the minute the bulb weakens. "Watch that one," they say. "It's about to blossom."

Could it be heaven does the same? The angels point to our bodies. The more frail we become, the more excited they become. "Watch that lady in the hospital," they say. "She's about to blossom." "Keep an eye on the fellow with the bad heart. He'll be coming home soon."

Traveling Light

God's View of Your Life

You are my place of safety and protection.
You are my God and I trust you.

PSALM 91:2

Have bad things *really* happened to you?
You and God may have different definitions
for the word *bad.* Parents and children do. Look
up the word *bad* in a middle-schooler's dictionary,
and you'll read definitions such as "pimple on nose,"
or "pop quiz in geometry." "Dad, this is really bad!"
the youngster says. Dad, having been around the
block a time or two, thinks differently. Pimples
pass. . . .

What you and I might rate as an absolute
disaster, God may rate as a pimple-level problem
that will pass. He views your life the way you view a
movie after you've read the book. When something
bad happens, you feel the air sucked out of the
theater. Everyone else gasps at the crisis on the
screen. Not you. Why? You've read the book. You
know how the good guy gets out of the tight spot.
God views your life with the same confidence.
He's not only read your story . . . he wrote it.

Come Thirsty

One Church, One Faith

"Holy Father, keep through Your name those whom
You have given Me, that they may be one as We are."

JOHN 17:11

 "May they all be one," Jesus prayed.
One. Not one in groups of two
thousand. But one in One. One church. One
faith. One Lord. Not Baptist, not Methodist,
not Adventist. Just Christians. No denominations.
No hierarchies. No traditions. Just Christ.

Too idealistic? Impossible to achieve? I don't
think so. Harder things have been done, you
know. For example, once upon a tree, a Creator
gave his life for his creation. Maybe all we need
are a few hearts that are willing to follow suit.

What about you? Can you build a bridge?
Toss a rope? Span a chasm? Pray for oneness?

No Wonder They Call Him the Savior

Store Up the Sweet

Whatever is true, whatever is honorable, . . . if there
is anything worthy of praise, think about these things.

PHILIPPIANS 4:8 RSV

Change the thoughts, and you change the
person. If today's thoughts are tomorrow's
actions, what happens when we fill our minds
with thoughts of God's love? Will standing beneath
the downpour of his grace change the way we feel
about others?

Paul says absolutely! It's not enough to keep
the bad stuff out. We've got to let the good stuff
in. It's not enough to keep no list of wrongs.
We have to cultivate a list of blessings: "Whatever
is true, whatever is honorable, whatever is just,
whatever is pure, whatever is lovely, whatever
is gracious, if there is any excellence, if there is
anything worthy of praise, think about these
things." *Thinking* conveys the idea of pondering—
studying and focusing, allowing what is viewed to
have an impact on us.

Rather than store up the sour, store up
the sweet.

A Love Worth Giving

Known for Humility

*Don't cherish exaggerated
ideas of yourself or your importance.*

ROMANS 12:3 PHILLIPS

The mightiest of the saints were known for their humility. Though Moses had served as prince of Egypt and emancipator of the slaves, the Bible says, "Moses was . . . more humble than anyone else" (Num. 12:3 NIV).

The apostle Paul was saved through a personal visit from Jesus. He was carried into the heavens and had the ability to raise the dead. But when he introduced himself, he mentioned none of these. He simply said, "I, Paul, am God's slave" (Titus 1:1 MSG).

John the Baptist was a blood relative of Jesus and the first evangelist in history, but he is remembered in Scripture as the one who resolved, "He must increase, but I must decrease" (John 3:30 NKJV).

Traveling Light

Nothing to Offer

LORD, I call to you. . . . Listen to me when I call to you.

PSALM 141:1

Nicodemus came to Jesus in the middle of the night. The centurion came in the middle of the day. The leper and the sinful woman appeared in the middle of crowds. Zacchaeus appeared in the middle of a tree. Matthew had a party for him.

The educated. The powerful. The rejected. The sick. The lonely. The wealthy. Who would have ever assembled such a crew? All they had in common were their empty hope chests, long left vacant by charlatans and profiteers. Though they had nothing to offer, they asked for everything: a new birth, a second chance, a fresh start, a clean conscience. And without exception their requests were honored.

Six Hours One Friday

Honest Worship

Take your everyday, ordinary life . . .
and place it before God as an offering.

ROMANS 12:1 MSG

Honest worship lifts eyes off self and sets them on God. Scripture's best-known worship leader wrote: "Give honor to the LORD, you angels; give honor to the LORD for his glory and strength. Give honor to the LORD for the glory of his name. Worship the LORD in the splendor of his holiness" (Ps. 29:1–2 NLT).

Worship gives God honor, offers him standing ovations.

We can make a big deal about God on Sundays with our songs and on Mondays with our strengths. Every day in every deed. Each time we do our best to thank God for giving his, we worship. "Take your everyday, ordinary life—your sleeping, eating, going-to-work, and walking-around life—and place it before God as an offering" (Rom. 12:1 MSG). Worship places God on center stage and us in proper posture.

Cure for the Common Life

A Positive Power

Death and life are in the power of the tongue.

PROVERBS 18:21 NKJV

Nathaniel Hawthorne came home heartbroken. He'd just been fired from his job in the custom house. His wife, rather than responding with anxiety, surprised him with joy. "Now you can write your book!"

He wasn't so positive. "And what shall we live on while I'm writing it?"

To his amazement she opened a drawer and revealed a wad of money she'd saved out of her housekeeping budget. "I always knew you were a man of genius," she told him. "I always knew you'd write a masterpiece."

She believed in her husband. And because she did, he wrote. And because he wrote, every library in America has a copy of *The Scarlet Letter* by Nathaniel Hawthorne.

You have the power to change someone's life simply by the words that you speak. "Death and life are in the power of the tongue."

A Love Worth Giving

Simplify Your Faith

"You have only one Master, the Christ."

MATTHEW 23:10

There are some who position themselves between you and God. There are some who suggest the only way to get to God is through them. There is the great teacher who has the final word on Bible teaching. There is the father who must bless your acts. There is the spiritual master who will tell you what God wants you to do. Jesus' message for complicated religion is to remove these middlemen. "You have only one Master, the Christ."

He's not saying that you don't need teachers, elders, or counselors. He is saying, however, that we are all brothers and sisters and have equal access to the Father. Simplify your faith by seeking God for yourself. No confusing ceremonies necessary. No mysterious rituals required. No elaborate channels of command or levels of access.

You have a Bible? You can study. You have a heart? You can pray. You have a mind? You can think.

And the Angels Were Silent

God's Poetry

We are His workmanship.

EPHESIANS 2:10 NKJV

Scripture calls the church a poem. "We are His workmanship" (Eph. 2:10). *Workmanship* descends from the Greek word *poeo* or *poetry*. We are God's poetry! What Longfellow did with pen and paper, our Maker does with us. We express his creative best.

You aren't God's poetry. I'm not God's poetry. *We* are God's poetry. Poetry demands variety. "God works through different men in different ways, but it is the same God who achieves his purposes through them all" (1 Cor. 12:6 PHILLIPS). God uses all types to type his message. Logical thinkers. Emotional worshipers. Dynamic leaders. Docile followers. The visionaries who lead, the studious who ponder, the generous who pay the bills. . . . Alone, we are meaningless symbols on a page. But collectively, we inspire.

Cure for the Common Life

The Christ of Your Mondays

I can do all things through Christ who strengthens me.

PHILIPPIANS 4:13 NKJV

Stand and consider:

- The Hubble Space Telescope sends back infrared images of faint galaxies that are perhaps twelve billion light-years away (twelve billion times six trillion miles).
- Astronomers venture a feeble estimate that the number of stars in the universe equals the number of grains of sand on all the beaches of the world.
- The star Betelgeuse has a diameter of 100 million miles, which is larger than the earth's orbit around the sun.

Why the immensity? Why such vast, unmeasured, unexplored, "unused" space? So that you and I, freshly stunned, could be stirred by this resolve: "I can do all things through Christ who strengthens me."

The Christ of the galaxies is the Christ of your Mondays.

Next Door Savior

He Cares About You

Anyone who is having troubles should pray.

JAMES 5:13

Have you taken your disappointments to God? You've shared them with your neighbor, your relatives, your friends. But have you taken them to God? James says, "Anyone who is having troubles should pray" (James 5:13).

Before you go anywhere else with your disappointments, go to God.

Maybe you don't want to trouble God with your hurts. *After all, he's got famines and pestilence and wars; he won't care about my little struggles,* you think. Why don't you let him decide that? He cared enough about a wedding to provide the wine. He cared enough about Peter's tax payment to give him a coin. He cared enough about the woman at the well to give her answers. "He cares about you" (1 Pet. 5:7).

Traveling Light

Run to Him!

His love has taken over our lives;
God's faithful ways are eternal.

PSALM 117:2, THE MESSAGE

God's love for you is not dependent on how you look, how you think, how you act, or how perfect you are. His love is absolutely nonnegotiable and nonreturnable. Ours is a faithful God.

No matter what you do, no matter how far you fall, no matter how ugly you become, God has a relentless, undying, unfathomable, unquenchable love from which you cannot be separated. Ever!

Run to Jesus. Jesus wants you to go to him. He wants to become the most important person in your life, the greatest love you'll ever know. He wants you to love him so much that there's no room in your heart and in your life for sin. Invite him to take up residence in your heart.

The Inspirational Study Bible

Working to Please God

*Work as if you were serving the Lord,
not as if you were serving only men and women.*

EPHESIANS 6:7

What if everyone worked with God in mind? Suppose no one worked to satisfy self or please the bottom line but everyone worked to please God.

Many occupations would instantly cease: drug trafficking, thievery, prostitution, nightclub and casino management. Certain careers, by their nature, cannot please God. These would cease.

Certain behaviors would cease as well. If I'm repairing a car for God, I'm not going to overcharge his children. If I'm painting a wall for God, you think I'm going to use paint thinner?

Imagine if everyone worked for the audience of One. Every nurse, thoughtful. Every officer, careful. Every professor, insightful. Every salesperson, delightful. Every teacher, hopeful. Every lawyer, skillful.

Impossible? Not entirely. All we need is someone to start a worldwide revolution. Might as well be us.

Cure for the Common Life

Filled to Overflowing

My cup overflows with blessings.

PSALM 23:5 NLT

The overflowing cup was a powerful symbol in the days of David. Hosts in the ancient East used it to send a message to the guest. As long as the cup was kept full, the guest knew he was welcome. But when the cup sat empty, the host was hinting that the hour was late. On those occasions, however, when the host really enjoyed the company of the person, he filled the cup to overflowing. He didn't stop when the wine reached the rim; he kept pouring until the liquid ran over the edge of the cup and down on the table.

Have you noticed how wet your table is? God wants you to stay. Your cup overflows with joy. Overflows with grace.

You have a place at God's table. And he is filling your cup to overflowing.

Traveling Light

Unfailing Love

"I will forgive them for leaving me and will love them freely."

HOSEA 14:4

Are you convinced that you have never lived a loveless day? Not one. Never unloved. Those times you deserted Christ? He loved you. You hid from him; he came looking for you.

And those occasions you denied Christ? Though you belonged to him, you hung with them, and when his name surfaced, you cursed like a drunken sailor. God let you hear the crowing of conscience and feel the heat of tears. But he never let you go. Your denials cannot diminish his love.

Nor can your doubts. You've had them. You may have them even now. While there is much we cannot know, may never know, can't we be sure of this? Doubts don't separate doubters from God's love.

Come Thirsty

Claiming Courage

You will teach me how to live a holy life.

PSALM 16:11

 Are you a brief journey away from painful encounters? Are you only steps away from the walls of your own heartache?

Learn a lesson from your master. Don't march into battle with the enemy without first claiming the courage from God's promises. May I give you a few examples?

When you are confused: "'I know what I am planning for you,' says the Lord. 'I have good plans for you, not plans to hurt you'" (Jer. 29:11 NCV).

If you feel weighted by yesterday's failures: "So now, those who are in Christ Jesus are not judged guilty" (Rom. 8:1 NCV).

On those nights when you wonder where God is: "I am the Holy One, and I am among you" (Hos. 11:9 NCV).

And the Angels Were Silent

September

God commands: . . .
that we love each other.

—1 John 3:23

The Power to Love

This is what God commands: . . . that we love each other.

Does bumping into certain people leave you brittle, breakable, and fruitless? Do you easily fall apart? If so, your love may be grounded in the wrong soil. It may be rooted in their love (which is fickle) or in your resolve to love (which is frail). John urges us to "rely on the love *God* has for us" (1 John 4:16 NIV, emphasis mine). He alone is the power source.

Many people tell us to love. Only God gives us the power to do so.

We know what God wants us to do. "This is what God commands: . . . that we love each other" (1 John 3:23). But how can we? How can we be kind to the vow breakers? To those who are unkind to us? How can we be patient with people who have the warmth of a vulture and the tenderness of a porcupine? How can we forgive the moneygrubbers and backstabbers we meet, love, and marry? How can we love as God loves? We want to. We long to. But how can we?

By living loved.

A Love Worth Giving

The Thorns of Sin

Evil people's lives are like
paths covered with thorns and traps.

PROVERBS 22:5

The fruit of sin is thorns—spiny, prickly, cutting thorns.

I emphasize the "point" of the thorns to suggest a point you may have never considered: If the fruit of sin is thorns, isn't the thorny crown on Christ's brow a picture of the fruit of our sin that pierced his heart?

What is the fruit of sin? Step into the briar patch of humanity and feel a few thistles. Shame. Fear. Disgrace. Discouragement. Anxiety. Haven't our hearts been caught in these brambles?

The heart of Jesus, however, had not. He had never been cut by the thorns of sin. What you and I face daily, he never knew. Anxiety? He never worried! Guilt? He was never guilty! Fear? He never left the presence of God! Jesus never knew the fruits of sin . . . until he became sin for us.

He Chose the Nails

Examine Your Tools

Kindle afresh the gift of God which is in you.

2 TIMOTHY 1:6 NASB

When I was six years old, my father built us a house. *Architectural Digest* didn't notice, but my mom sure did. Dad constructed it, board by board, every day after work. My youth didn't deter him from giving me a job. He tied an empty nail apron around my waist, placed a magnet in my hands, and sent me on daily patrols around the building site, carrying my magnet only inches off the ground.

One look at my tools and you could guess my job. Stray-nail collector.

One look at yours and the same can be said. Brick by brick, life by life, God is creating a kingdom, a "spiritual house" (1 Pet. 2:5 CEV). He entrusted you with a key task in the project. Examine your tools and discover it. Your ability unveils your destiny.

Cure for the Common Life

Dare to Dream

God can do things that are not possible for people to do.

LUKE 18:27

God always rejoices when we dare to dream. In fact, we are much like God when we dream. The Master exults in newness. He delights in stretching the old. He wrote the book on making the impossible possible.

Examples? Check the Book.

Eighty-year-old shepherds don't usually play chicken with Pharaohs . . . but don't tell that to Moses.

Teenage shepherds don't normally have showdowns with giants . . . but don't tell that to David.

Night-shift shepherds don't usually get to hear angels sing and see God in a stable . . . but don't tell that to the Bethlehem bunch.

And for sure don't tell that to God. He's made an eternity out of making the earthbound airborne. And he gets angry when people's wings are clipped.

And the Angels Were Silent

He Weeps with Us

Jesus wept.

JOHN 11:35 NKJV

Jesus . . . weeps. He sits between Mary and Martha, puts an arm around each, and sobs. . . .

He weeps with them.
He weeps for them.
He weeps with you.
He weeps for you.

He weeps so we will know: Mourning is not disbelieving. Flooded eyes don't represent a faithless heart. A person can enter a cemetery Jesus-certain of life after death and still have a Twin Tower crater in the heart. Christ did. He wept, and he knew he was ten minutes from seeing a living Lazarus!

And his tears give you permission to shed your own. Grief does not mean you don't trust; it simply means you can't stand the thought of another day without the Lazarus of your life. If Jesus gave the love, he understands the tears. So grieve, but don't grieve like those who don't know the rest of this story.

Next Door Savior

Heaven Knows Your Heart

Naked a man comes from his mother's womb,
and as he comes, so he departs.

ECCLESIASTES 5:15 NIV

Think for just a moment about the things you own. Think about the house you have, the car you drive, the money you've saved. Think about the stocks you've traded and the clothes you've purchased. Envision all your stuff, and let me remind you of two biblical truths.

Your stuff isn't yours. Ask any coroner. . . . No one takes anything with him. When one of the wealthiest men in history, John D. Rockefeller, died, his accountant was asked, "How much did John D. leave?" The accountant's reply? "All of it."

All that stuff—it's not yours. And you know what else about all that stuff? *It's not you.* Who you are has nothing to do with the clothes you wear or the car you drive. Jesus said, "Life is not defined by what you have, even when you have a lot" (Luke 12:15 MSG). Heaven does not know you as the fellow with the nice suit or the woman with the big house or the kid with the new bike. Heaven knows your heart.

Traveling Light

Love Is Patient

Let your patience show itself perfectly in what you do.

JAMES 1:4

Sometime ago our church staff attended a leadership conference. Especially interested in one class, I arrived early and snagged a front-row seat. As the speaker began, however, I was distracted by a couple of voices in the back of the room. Two guys were mumbling to each other. I was giving serious thought to shooting a glare over my shoulder when the speaker offered an explanation. "Forgive me," he said. "I forgot to explain why the two fellows at the back of the class are talking. One of them is an elder at a new church in Romania. He has traveled here to learn about church leadership. But he doesn't speak English, so the message is being translated."

All of a sudden everything changed. Patience replaced impatience. Why? Because patience always hitches a ride with understanding. "A man of understanding holds his tongue" (Prov. 11:12 NIV). Don't miss the connection between understanding and patience. Before you blow up, listen up. Before you strike out, tune in.

A Love Worth Giving

The Reality of Faith

"Surely this was a righteous man."

LUKE 23:47 NIV

If it is true that a picture paints a thousand words, then there was a Roman centurion who got a dictionary full. All he did was see Jesus suffer. He never heard him preach or saw him heal or followed him through the crowds. He never witnessed him still the wind; he only witnessed the way he died. But that was all it took to cause this weather-worn soldier to take a giant step in faith. "Surely this was a righteous man."

That says a lot, doesn't it? It says the rubber of faith meets the road of reality under hardship. It says the trueness of one's belief is revealed in pain. Genuineness and character are unveiled in misfortune. Faith is at its best, not in three-piece suits on Sunday mornings or at V.B.S. on summer days, but at hospital bedsides, cancer wards, and cemeteries.

No Wonder They Call Him the Savior

The Departure Date

*Your life is like a mist. You can see it
for a short time, but then it goes away.*

JAMES 4:14

You, as all God's children, live one final
breath from your own funeral.

Which, from God's perspective, is nothing to
grieve. He responds to these grave facts with this
great news: "The day you die is better than the
day you are born" (Eccles. 7:1 NLT). Now there is
a twist. Heaven enjoys a maternity-ward reaction
to funerals. Angels watch body burials the same
way grandparents monitor delivery-room doors.
"He'll be coming through any minute!" They can't
wait to see the new arrival. While we're driving
hearses and wearing black, they're hanging pink
and blue streamers and passing out cigars. We
don't grieve when babies enter the world. The
hosts of heaven don't weep when we leave it.

Come Thirsty

Is It Loving?

[Love] is not rude.

1 CORINTHIANS 13:5 NIV

When defining what love is not, Paul put *rudeness* on the list. "It is not rude." The Greek word for *rude* means shameful or disgraceful behavior.

An example of rudeness was recently taken before the courts in Minnesota. A man fell out of his canoe and lost his temper. Though the river was lined with vacationing families, he polluted the air with obscenities. Some of those families sued him. He said, "I have my rights."

God calls us to a higher, more noble concern. Not "What are my rights?" but "What is loving?"

Do you have the right to dominate a conversation? Yes, but is it loving to do so? . . .

Is it within your rights to bark at the clerk or snap at the kids? Yes. But is it loving to act this way?

A Love Worth Giving

An Open Door

*Now in Christ Jesus, you who were
far away from God are brought near.*

EPHESIANS 2:13

Nothing remains between you and God
but an open door.

Something happened in the death of Christ
that opened the door for you and me. And that
something is described by the writer of Hebrews.

"So, brothers and sisters, we are completely
free to enter the Most Holy Place without fear
because of the blood of Jesus' death. We can enter
through a new and living way that Jesus opened
for us. It leads through the curtain—Christ's body"
(Heb. 10:19–20).

To the original readers, those last four words
were explosive: "the curtain—Christ's body."
According to the writer, the curtain equals Jesus.
Hence, whatever happened to the flesh of Jesus
happened to the curtain. What happened to his
flesh? It was torn. Torn by the whips, torn by the
thorns. Torn by the weight of the cross and the
point of the nails. But in the horror of his torn
flesh, we find the splendor of the open door.

He Chose the Nails

Too Incredible

The One who comes from above is greater than all.

JOHN 3:31

The idea that a virgin would be selected by God to bear himself. . . . The notion that God would don a scalp and toes and two eyes. . . . The thought that the King of the universe would sneeze and burp and get bit by mosquitoes. . . . It's too incredible. Too revolutionary. We would never create such a Savior. We aren't that daring.

When we create a redeemer, we keep him safely distant in his faraway castle. We allow him only the briefest of encounters with us. We permit him to swoop in and out with his sleigh before we can draw too near. We wouldn't ask him to take up residence in the midst of a contaminated people. In our wildest imaginings we wouldn't conjure a king who becomes one of us.

But God did.

And the Angels Were Silent

The Lamb of God

*At noon the whole country was covered
with darkness, which lasted for three hours.*

MATTHEW 27:45 TEV

Of course the sky is dark; people are killing
the Light of the World.

The universe grieves. God said it would. "On
that day . . . I will make the sun go down at noon,
and darken the earth in broad daylight. . . . I will
make it like the mourning for an only son, and
the end of it like a bitter day" (Amos 8:9–10 RSV).

The sky weeps. And a lamb bleats. Remember
the time of the scream? "At about three o'clock
Jesus cried out." Three o'clock in the afternoon,
the hour of the temple sacrifice. Less than a mile
to the east, a finely clothed priest leads a lamb to
the slaughter, unaware that his work is futile.
Heaven is not looking at the lamb of man but at
"the Lamb of God, who takes away the sin of the
world" (John 1:29 RSV).

Next Door Savior

A Second Chance

"I came to give life—life in all its fullness."

Not many second chances exist in the world today. Just ask the kid who didn't make the little league team or the fellow who got the pink slip or the mother of three who got dumped for a "pretty little thing."

Not many second chances. Nowadays it's more like, "It's now or never." "Around here we don't tolerate incompetence." "Gotta get tough to get along." "Not much room at the top." "Three strikes and you're out." "It's a dog-eat-dog world!"

Jesus . . . would say. "Then don't live with the dogs." That makes sense doesn't it? Why let a bunch of other failures tell you how much of a failure you are? . . .

It's not every day that you find someone who will give you a second chance—much less someone who will give you a second chance every day. But in Jesus, you find both.

No Wonder They Call Him the Savior

Obsessed with Stuff

Be on your guard against every form of greed.

LUKE 12:15 NASB

In 1900 the average person living in the United States wanted seventy-two different things and considered eighteen of them essential. Today the average person wants five hundred things and considers one hundred of them essential.

Our obsession with stuff carries a hefty price tag. Eighty percent of us battle the pressure of overdue bills. We spend 110 percent of our disposable income trying to manage debt. And who can keep up? We no longer measure ourselves against the Joneses next door but against the star on the screen or the stud on the magazine cover. Hollywood's diamonds make yours look like a gumball-machine toy. Who can satisfy Madison Avenue? No one can. For that reason Jesus warns, "Be on your guard against every form of greed" (Luke 12:15 NASB).

Cure for the Common Life

A Symbol of Love

He is not here; he has risen from the dead.

LUKE 24:6

When John arrived at the empty tomb the burial wraps had not been ripped off and thrown down. They were still in their original state! The linens were undisturbed. The graveclothes were still rolled and folded.

How could this be? . . .

If for some reason friends or foes had unwrapped the body, would they have been so careful as to dispose of the clothing in such an orderly fashion? Of course not! But if neither friend nor foe took the body, who did? . . .

Through the rags of death, John saw the power of life. Odd, don't you think, that God would use something as sad as a burial wrap to change a life?

But God is given to such practices:

In his hand empty wine jugs at a wedding become a symbol of power.

The coin of a widow becomes a symbol of generosity.

And a tool of death is a symbol of his love.

He Chose the Nails

The Pot of Prayer

I will go to the altar of God,
to God who is my joy and happiness.

PSALM 43:4

Let's say a stress stirrer comes your way. The doctor decides you need an operation. She detects a lump and thinks it best that you have it removed. So there you are, walking out of her office. You've just been handed this cup of anxiety. What are you going to do with it? You can place it in one of two pots.

You can dump your bad news in the vat of worry and pull out the spoon. Turn on the fire. Stew on it. Stir it. Mope for a while. Brood for a time. Won't be long before you'll have a delightful pot of pessimism.

How about a different idea? The pot of prayer. Before the door of the doctor's office closes, give the problem to God. "I receive your lordship. Nothing comes to me that hasn't passed through you." In addition, stir in a healthy helping of gratitude.

Your part is prayer and gratitude. God's part? Peace and protection.

Come Thirsty

Jesus Planned It All

"Look, the Lamb of God,
who takes away the sin of the world!"

JOHN 1:29

Jesus planned his own sacrifice.

It means Jesus intentionally planted the tree from which his cross would be carved.

It means he willingly placed the iron ore in the heart of the earth from which the nails would be cast.

It means he voluntarily placed his Judas in the womb of a woman.

It means Christ was the one who set in motion the political machinery that would send Pilate to Jerusalem.

And it also means he didn't have to do it—but he did.

God Came Near

Submerged in Mercy

> [God] has not punished us
> as our sins should be punished.
>
> PSALM 103:10

Do you really think you haven't done things that hurt Christ?

Have you ever been dishonest with his money? That's cheating.

Ever gone to church to be seen rather than to see him? Hypocrite.

Ever broken a promise you've made to God?

Don't you deserve to be punished? And yet, here you are. Reading this book. Breathing. Still witnessing sunsets and hearing babies gurgle. Still watching the seasons change. There are no lashes on your back or hooks in your nose or shackles on your feet. Apparently God hasn't kept a list of your wrongs.

Listen. You have not been sprinkled with forgiveness. You have not been spattered with grace. You have not been dusted with kindness. You have been immersed in it. You are submerged in mercy. You are a minnow in the ocean of his mercy. Let it change you!

A Love Worth Giving

A Pasture for the Soul

He lets me rest in green pastures.

PSALM 23:2

For a field to bear fruit, it must occasionally lie fallow. And for you to be healthy, you must rest. Slow down, and God will heal you. He will bring rest to your mind, to your body, and most of all to your soul. He will lead you to green pastures.

Green pastures were not the natural terrain of Judea. The hills around Bethlehem where David kept his flock were not lush and green. Even today they are white and parched. Any green pasture in Judea is the work of some shepherd. He has cleared the rough, rocky land. Stumps have been torn out, and brush has been burned. . . .

With his own pierced hands, Jesus created a pasture for the soul. He tore out the thorny underbrush of condemnation. He pried loose the huge boulders of sin. In their place he planted seeds of grace and dug ponds of mercy.

And he invites us to rest there.

Traveling Light

At Home with His Love

"Abide in My love."

JOHN 15:9 NASB

When you abide somewhere, you live there. You grow familiar with the surroundings. You don't pull in the driveway and ask, "Where is the garage?" You don't consult the blueprint to find the kitchen. To abide is to be at home.

To abide in Christ's love is to make his love your home. Not a roadside park or hotel room you occasionally visit, but your preferred dwelling. You rest in him. Eat in him. When thunder claps, you step beneath his roof. His walls secure you from the winds. His fireplace warms you from the winters of life. As John urged, "We take up permanent residence in a life of love" (1 John 4:16 MSG).

You abandon the old house of false love and move into his home of real love.

Come Thirsty

"God Is for Me"

You number my wanderings; put my tears into Your bottle.

PSALM 56:8 NKJV

God knows you. He engraved your name on his hands and keeps your tears in a bottle (Isa. 49:16; Ps. 56:8). . . .

God knows you. And he is near you! How far is the shepherd from the sheep (John 10:14)? The branch from the vine (John 15:5)? That's how far God is from you. He is near. See how these four words look taped to your bathroom mirror: "God is for me" (Ps. 56:9 NKJV).

And his kingdom needs you. The poor need you; the lonely need you; the church needs you . . . the cause of God needs you. You are part of "the overall purpose he is working out in everything and everyone" (Eph. 1:11 MSG). The kingdom needs you to discover and deploy your unique skill. Use it to make much out of God. Get the word out. God is with us; we are not alone.

Cure for the Common Life

Refuse Trashy Thoughts

As he thinks in his heart, so is he.

PROVERBS 23:7 NKJV

To listen to our vocabulary you'd think we are the victims of our thoughts. "Don't talk to me," we say. "I'm in a bad mood." As if a mood were a place to which we were assigned ("I can't call you. I'm in Bosnia.") rather than an emotion we permit.

Or we say, "Don't mess with her. She has a bad disposition." Is a disposition something we "have"? Like a cold or the flu? Are we the victims of the emotional bacteria of the season? Or do we have a choice?

Paul says we do: "We capture every thought and make it give up and obey Christ" (2 Cor. 10:5).

Do you hear some battlefield jargon in that passage—"capture every thought," "make it give up" and "obey Christ"? You get the impression that we are the soldiers and the thoughts are the enemies. Our assignment is to protect the boat and refuse entrance to trashy thoughts. The minute they appear . . . we go into action. "This heart belongs to God," we declare, "and you aren't getting on board."

A Love Worth Giving

Get Over Yourself

In humility consider others better than yourselves.

PHILIPPIANS 2:3 NIV

Columnist Rick Reilly gave this advice to rookie professional athletes: "Stop thumping your chest. The line blocked, the quarterback threw you a perfect spiral while getting his head knocked off, and the good receiver blew the double coverage. Get over yourself."

The truth is, every touchdown in life is a team effort. Applaud your teammates. An elementary-age boy came home from the tryouts for the school play. "Mommy, Mommy," he announced, "I got a part. I've been chosen to sit in the audience and clap and cheer." When you have a chance to clap and cheer, do you take it? If you do, your head is starting to fit your hat size.

Traveling Light

Go the Distance

"Those people who keep their faith
until the end will be saved."

MATTHEW 24:13

Jesus doesn't say if you succeed you will be saved. Or if you come out on top you will be saved. He says if you endure. An accurate rendering would be, "If you hang in there until the end . . . if you go the distance."

The Brazilians have a great phrase for this. In Portuguese, a person who has the ability to hang in and not give up has *garra*. *Garra* means "claws." What imagery! A person with *garra* has claws that burrow into the side of the cliff and keep him from falling.

So do the saved. They may get close to the edge; they may even stumble and slide. But they will dig their nails into the rock of God and hang on.

Jesus gives you this assurance. Hang on. He'll make sure you get home.

And the Angels Were Silent

A Place to Heal

Christ gave those gifts to prepare God's holy people for the work of serving, to make the body of Christ stronger.

EPHESIANS 4:11–12

He grants gifts so we can "*prepare* God's holy people." Paul reached into a medical dictionary for this term. Doctors used it to describe the setting of a broken bone. Broken people come to churches. Not with broken bones, but broken hearts, homes, dreams, and lives. They limp in on fractured faith, and if the church operates as the church, they find healing. Pastor-teachers touch and teach. Gospel bearers share good news. Prophets speak words of truth. Visionaries dream of greater impact. Some administer. Some pray. Some lead. Some follow. But all help to heal brokenness: "to make the body of Christ stronger."

Don't miss it. No one is strong all the time. Don't miss the place to find your place and heal your hurts.

Cure for the Common Life

God Goes with Us

*"I am with you and will
watch over you wherever you go."*

GENESIS 28:15 NIV

When God calls us into the deep valley
of death, he will be with us. Dare we think
that he would abandon us in the moment of
death? . . . Would the shepherd require his sheep
to journey to the highlands alone? Of course not.
Would God require his child to journey to eternity
alone? Absolutely not! He is with you!

What God said to Moses, he says to you:
"My Presence will go with you, and I will give
you rest" (Exod. 33:14 NIV).

What God said to Jacob, he says to you:
"I am with you and will watch over you wherever
you go" (Gen. 28:15 NIV).

What God said to Joshua, he says to you:
"As I was with Moses, so I will be with you; I will
never leave you nor forsake you" (Josh. 1:5 NIV).

Traveling Light

Receive God's Hope

Come near to God and God will come near to you.

Your toughest challenge is nothing more than bobby pins and rubber bands to God. *Bobby pins and rubber bands?*

My older sister used to give them to me when I was a child. I would ride my tricycle up and down the sidewalk, pretending that the bobby pins were keys and my trike was a truck. But one day I lost the "keys." Crisis! What was I going to do? My search yielded nothing but tears and fear. But when I confessed my mistake to my sister, she just smiled. Being a decade older, she had a better perspective.

God has a better perspective as well. With all due respect, our severest struggles are, in his view, nothing worse than lost bobby pins and rubber bands. He is not confounded, confused, or discouraged.

Receive his hope, won't you? Receive it because you need it. Receive it so you can share it.

A Love Worth Giving

Six Hours One Friday

"He really was the Son of God!"

MATTHEW 27:54

To the casual observer the six hours are mundane. . . .

God is on a cross. The creator of the universe is being executed.

Spit and blood are caked to his cheeks, and his lips are cracked and swollen. Thorns rip his scalp. His lungs scream with pain. His legs knot with cramps. Taut nerves threaten to snap as pain twangs her morbid melody. Yet, death is not ready. And there is no one to save him, for he is sacrificing himself.

It is no normal six hours . . . it is no normal Friday.

Let me ask you a question: What do you do with that day in history? What do you do with its claims?

If it really happened . . . if God did commandeer his own crucifixion . . . if he did turn his back on his own son . . . those six hours were no normal six hours. They were the most critical hours in history.

Six Hours One Friday

Uniquely You

He gave . . . to each according to his ability.

MATTHEW 25:15 NKJV

Da Vinci painted one *Mona Lisa*. Beethoven composed one Fifth Symphony. And God made one version of you. He custom designed you for a one-of-a-kind assignment. Mine like a gold digger the unique-to-you nuggets from your life. . . .

When God gives an assignment, he also gives the skill. Study your skills, then, to reveal your assignment.

Look at you. Your uncanny ease with numbers. Your quenchless curiosity about chemistry. Others stare at blueprints and yawn; you read them and drool. "I was made to do this," you say.

Our Maker gives assignments to people, "to each according to each one's unique ability." As he calls, he equips. Look back over your life. What have you consistently done well? What have you loved to do? Stand at the intersection of your affections and successes and find your uniqueness.

Cure for the Common Life

October

We can come before God's throne
where there is grace.

—Hebrews 4:16

Is That All There Is?

Christ died for our sins in accordance with the scriptures.

1 CORINTHIANS 15:3 NIV

Maybe you've gone through the acts of religion and faith and yet found yourself more often than not at a dry well. Prayers seem empty. Goals seem unthinkable. Christianity becomes a warped record full of highs and lows and off-key notes.

Is this all there is? Sunday attendance. Pretty songs. Faithful tithings. Golden crosses. Three-piece suits. Big choirs. Leather Bibles. It is nice and all, but . . . where is the heart of it? . . .

Think about these words from Paul in 1 Corinthians, chapter 15. "For I delivered to you as of first importance what I also received, that Christ died for our sins in accordance with the scriptures" (NIV).

There it is. Almost too simple. Jesus was killed, buried, and resurrected. Surprised? The part that matters is the cross. No more and no less.

No Wonder They Call Him the Savior

A Personal Invitation

"Come to me . . . and I will give you rest."

MATTHEW 11:28

When Jesus says, "Come to me," he doesn't say come to religion, come to a system, or come to a certain doctrine. This is a very personal invitation to a God, an invitation to a Savior.

Our God is not aloof—he's not so far above us that he can't see and understand our problems. Jesus isn't a God who stayed on the mountaintop— he's a Savior who came down and lived and worked with the people. Everywhere he went, the crowds followed, drawn together by the magnet that was— and is—the Savior.

The life of Jesus Christ is a message of hope, a message of mercy, a message of life in a dark world.

The Inspirational Study Bible

The Journey to the Cross

This was God's plan which he had made long ago;
he knew all this would happen.

ACTS 2:23

Jesus died . . . on purpose. No surprise. No hesitation. No faltering.

You can tell a lot about a person by the way he dies. And the way Jesus marched to his death leaves no doubt: he had come to earth for this moment. Read the words of Peter. "Jesus was given to you, and with the help of those who don't know the law, you put him to death by nailing him to a cross. But this was God's plan which he had made long ago; he knew all this would happen" (Acts 2:23 NCV).

No, the journey to the cross didn't begin in Jericho. It didn't begin in Galilee. It didn't begin in Nazareth. It didn't even begin in Bethlehem.

The journey to the cross began long before. As the echo of the crunching of the fruit was still sounding in the garden, Jesus was leaving for Calvary.

And the Angels Were Silent

An Uncommon Call

*The Spirit has given each of us a
special way of serving others.*

1 Corinthians 2:7 CEV

You have one. A divine spark. An
uncommon call to an uncommon life.
"The Spirit has given each of us a *special way* of
serving others." So much for the excuse "I don't
have anything to offer." Did the apostle Paul say,
"The Spirit has given *some* of us . . ."? Or, "The
Spirit has given *a few* of us . . ."? No. "The Spirit
has given *each of us* a special way of serving
others." Enough of this self-deprecating "I can't
do anything."

And enough of its arrogant opposite: "I have
to do everything." No, you don't! You're not God's
solution to society, but a solution in society. Imitate
Paul, who said, "Our goal is to stay within the
boundaries of God's plan for us" (2 Cor. 10:13 NLT).
Clarify your contribution.

Don't worry about skills you don't have.
Don't covet strengths others do have. Just extract
your uniqueness.

Cure for the Common Life

He Was Reachable

The Word became flesh and dwelt among us.

JOHN 1:14 NKJV

"The Word became flesh," John said.

In other words . . . he was touchable, approachable, reachable. And, what's more, he was ordinary. If he were here today you probably wouldn't notice him as he walked through a shopping mall. He wouldn't turn heads by the clothes he wore or the jewelry he flashed.

"Just call me Jesus," you can almost hear him say.

He was the kind of fellow you'd invite to watch the Rams-Giants game at your house. He'd wrestle on the floor with your kids, doze on your couch, and cook steaks on your grill. He'd laugh at your jokes and tell a few of his own. And when you spoke, he'd listen to you as if he had all the time in eternity.

And one thing's for sure, you'd invite him back.

God Came Near

A Finished Work

God began doing a good work in you,
and I am sure he will continue it until it is finished.

PHILIPPIANS 1:6

The message of Jesus to the religious person is simple: It's not what you do. It's what I do. I have moved in.

Religious rule-keeping can sap your strength. It's endless. There is always another class to attend, Sabbath to obey, Ramadan to observe. No prison is as endless as the prison of perfection. Her inmates find work but never find peace. How could they? They never know when they are finished.

Christ, however, gifts you with a finished work. He fulfilled the law for you. Bid farewell to the burden of religion. Gone is the fear that having done everything, you might not have done enough. You climb the stairs, not by your strength, but his. God pledges to help those who stop trying to help themselves.

Next Door Savior

Everything You Need

My God will use his wonderful riches
in Christ Jesus to give you everything you need.

PHILIPPIANS 4:19

May I meddle for a moment? What is the one thing separating you from joy? How do you fill in this blank: "I will be happy when _____"? When I am healed. When I am promoted. When I am married. When I am single. When I am rich. How would you finish that statement?

Now, with your answer firmly in mind, answer this. If your ship never comes in, if your dream never comes true, if the situation never changes, could you be happy? If not, then you . . . need to know what you have in your Shepherd.

You have a God who hears you, the power of love behind you, the Holy Spirit within you, and all of heaven ahead of you. If you have the Shepherd, you have grace for every sin, direction for every turn, a candle for every corner, and an anchor for every storm. You have everything you need.

Traveling Light

Our Courteous Christ

The Son of Man did not come to be served, but to serve.

MARK 10:45 NKJV

I had never thought much about the courtesy of Christ before, but as I began looking, I realized that Jesus makes Emily Post look like Archie Bunker.

He always knocks before entering. He doesn't have to. He owns your heart. If anyone has the right to barge in, Christ does. But he doesn't. That gentle tap you hear? It's Christ. "Behold, I stand at the door and knock" (Rev. 3:20 NASB). And when you answer, he awaits your invitation to cross the threshold. . . .

And when he enters, he always brings a gift. Some bring Chianti and daisies. Christ brings "the gift of the Holy Spirit" (Acts 2:38). And, as he stays, he serves. "For even the Son of Man did not come to be served, but to serve" (Mark 10:45 NIV). If you're missing your apron, you'll find it on him. He's serving the guests as they sit (John 13:4–5). He won't eat until he's offered thanks, and he won't leave until the leftovers are put away (Matt. 14:19–20).

A Love Worth Giving

Jesus Dispels Doubt

*They were fearful and terrified . . . but Jesus said,
"Why are you troubled? . . . It is I myself!"*

LUKE 24:37–38

They had betrayed their Master. When
Jesus needed them they had scampered.
And now they were having to deal with the shame.

Seeking forgiveness, but not knowing where
to look for it, the disciples came back. They
gravitated to that same upper room that contained
the sweet memories of broken bread and
symbolic wine. . . .

They came back. Each with a scrapbook full
of memories and a thin thread of hope. Each
knowing that it is all over, but in his heart
hoping that the impossible will happen once
more. "If I had just one more chance." . . .

And just when the gloom gets good and
thick, just when their wishful thinking is falling
victim to logic, just when someone says, "How I'd
give my immortal soul to see him one more time,"
a familiar face walks through the wall.

My, what an ending. Or, better said, what
a beginning!

No Wonder They Call Him the Savior

Help from the Holy Spirit

The Spirit comes to the aid of our weakness.

ROMANS 8:26 NEB

 *The Spirit comes to the aid of our weakness.*
What a sentence worthy of a highlighter.
Who does not need this reminder? Weak bodies.
Weak wills. Weakened resolves. We've known
them all. The word *weakness* can refer to physical
infirmities, as with the invalid who had been
unable to walk for thirty-eight years (John 5:5),
or spiritual impotence, as with the spiritually
"helpless" of Romans 5:6.

Whether we are feeble of soul or body or
both, how good to know it's not up to us.
The Spirit himself is pleading for us.

Come Thirsty

You Can Trust Him

We can come before God's throne where there is grace.
There we receive mercy . . . to help us when we need it.

Why did Jesus live on the earth as long as he did? Couldn't his life have been much shorter? Why not step into our world just long enough to die for our sins and then leave? Why not a sinless year or week? Why did he have to live a life? To take on our sins is one thing, but to take on our sunburns, our sore throats? To experience death, yes—but to put up with life? To put up with long roads, long days, and short tempers? Why did he do it?

Because he wants you to trust him. . . .

He has been where you are and can relate to how you feel. And if his life on earth doesn't convince you, his death on the cross should. He understands what you are going through. Our Lord does not patronize us or scoff at our needs. He responds "generously to all without finding fault" (James 1:5 NIV).

He Chose the Nails

Religion by Computer

Those who believe in the Son have eternal life.

JOHN 3:36

Computerized Christianity. Push the right buttons, enter the right code, insert the correct data, and bingo, print out your own salvation.

You do your part and the Divine Computer does his. No need to pray (after all, you control the keyboard). No emotional attachment necessary (who wants to hug circuits?). And worship? Well, worship is a lab exercise—insert the rituals and see the results.

Religion by computer. That's what happens when . . .

you replace the living God with a cold system;

you replace inestimable love with pro-forma budget;

you replace the ultimate sacrifice of Christ with the puny achievements of man.

And the Angels Were Silent

Jesus Resisted Temptation

*He was tempted in every way that
we are, but he did not sin.*

Hebrews 4:15

When his accusers called him a servant of
Satan, Jesus demanded to see their
evidence. "Which one of you convicts Me of sin?"
he dared (John 8:46 NASB). Ask my circle of
friends to point out my sin, and watch the hands
shoot up. When those who knew Jesus were asked
this same question, no one spoke. Christ was
followed by disciples, analyzed by crowds, criticized
by family, and scrutinized by enemies, yet not one
person would remember him committing even one
sin. He was never found in the wrong place. Never
said the wrong word. Never acted the wrong way.
He never sinned. Not that he wasn't tempted, mind
you. He was "tempted in every way that we are,
but he did not sin."

Lust wooed him. Greed lured him. Power
called him. Jesus—the human—was tempted.
But Jesus—the holy God—resisted.

Next Door Savior

An Act of Grace

"I lay down my life for the sheep."

JOHN 10:15 NIV

Our Master lived a three-dimensional life. He had as clear a view of the future as he did of the present and the past.

This is why the ropes used to tie his hands and the soldiers used to lead him to the cross were unnecessary. They were incidental. Had they not been there, had there been no trial, no Pilate and no crowd, the very same crucifixion would have occurred. Had Jesus been forced to nail himself to the cross, he would have done it. For it was not the soldiers who killed him, nor the screams of the mob: It was his devotion to us.

So call it what you wish: an act of grace; a plan of redemption; a martyr's sacrifice. But whatever you call it, don't call it an accident. It was anything but that.

God Came Near

Take Risks for God

"Well done good and faithful servant;
you were faithful over a few things, I will make
you ruler over many things."

MATTHEW 25:21 NKJV

Use your uniqueness to take great risks for God!

If you're great with kids, volunteer at the orphanage.

If you have a head for business, start a soup kitchen.

If God bent you toward medicine, dedicate a day or a decade to AIDS patients.

The only mistake is not to risk making one. . . .

He lavished you with strengths in this life and a promise of the next. Go out on a limb; he won't let you fall. Take a big risk; he won't let you fail. He invites you to dream of the day you feel his hand on your shoulder and his eyes on your face. "Well done," he will say, "good and faithful servant."

Cure for the Common Life

Absurdities and Ironies

"Father, into your hands I commit My spirit."

LUKE 23:46 NKJV

As Christ gave his final breath, the earth gave a sudden stir. A rock rolled, and a soldier stumbled. Then, as suddenly as the silence was broken, the silence returned. And now all is quiet. The mocking has ceased. There is no one to mock.

The soldiers are busy with the business of cleaning up the dead. Two men have come. Dressed well and meaning well, they are given the body of Jesus.

And we are left with the relics of his death.

Three nails in a bin.

Three cross-shaped shadows.

A braided crown with scarlet tips.

Bizarre, isn't it? The thought that this blood is not man's blood but God's?

Crazy, isn't it? To think that these nails held your sins to a cross? . . .

Absurdities and ironies. The hill of Calvary is nothing if not both.

He Chose the Nails

God's Mighty Angels

*The angels are spirits who serve God and
are sent to help those who will receive salvation.*

HEBREWS 1:14

Chiffon wings and meringue sweetness?
Perhaps for angels in the gift books and
specialty shops, but God's angels are marked by
indescribable strength. Paul says Christ "will come
with his mighty angels" (2 Thess. 1:7 NLT). From
the word translated *mighty*, we have the English
word *dynamic*. Angels pack dynamic force. It took
only one angel to slay the firstborn of Egypt
and only one angel to close the mouths of the
lions to protect Daniel. David called angels "mighty
creatures who carry out his plans, listening for
each of his commands" (Ps. 103:20 NLT).

No need for you to talk to angels; they won't
listen. Their ears incline only to God's voice.
They are "spirits who serve God," responding to
his command and following only his directions.
Jesus said they "always see the face of my Father
in heaven" (Matt. 18:10 NIV). Only one sound
matters to angels—God's voice.

Come Thirsty

Room for Miracles

"I will not believe it until I see the nail marks in his hands and . . . put my hand into his side."

In our world of budgets, long-range planning and computers, don't we find it hard to trust in the unbelievable? Don't most of us tend to scrutinize life behind furrowed brows and walk with cautious steps? It's hard for us to imagine that God can surprise us. To make a little room for miracles today, well, it's not sound thinking.

We make the same mistake that Thomas made: we forget that "impossible" is one of God's favorite words.

How about you? How is your imagination these days? When was the last time you let some of your dreams elbow out your logic? When was the last time you imagined the unimaginable? . . . Has it been awhile since you claimed God's promise to do "more than we can ask or imagine?" (Eph. 3:20)

No Wonder They Call Him the Savior

Love Rejoices in Truth

Love does not delight in evil but rejoices with the truth.

1 CORINTHIANS 13:6 NIV

In this verse lies a test for love.

Here's an example. A classic one. A young couple are on a date. His affection goes beyond her comfort zone. She resists. But he tries to persuade her with the oldest line in the book: "But I love you. I just want to be near you. If you loved me . . ."

That siren you hear? It's the phony-love detector. This guy doesn't love her. . . . He may love her body. He may love boasting to his buddies about his conquest. But he doesn't love her. True love will never ask the "beloved" to do what he or she thinks is wrong. . . .

Do you want to know if your love for someone is true? If your friendship is genuine? . . . Ask yourself: Do I influence this person to do what is right?

A Love Worth Giving

Fretting Is Futile

*You cannot add any time
to your life by worrying about it.*

MATTHEW 6:27

No one has to remind you of the high cost of anxiety. (But I will anyway.) Worry divides the mind. The biblical word for *worry* (*merimnao*) is a compound of two Greek words, *merizo* ("to divide") and *nous* ("the mind"). Anxiety splits our energy between today's priorities and tomorrow's problems. Part of our mind is on the now; the rest is on the not yet. The result is half-minded living.

That's not the only result. Worrying is not a disease, but it causes diseases. It has been connected to high blood pressure, heart trouble, blindness, migraine headaches, thyroid malfunctions, and a host of stomach disorders.

Anxiety is an expensive habit. Of course, it might be worth the cost if it worked. But it doesn't. Our frets are futile. Worry has never brightened a day, solved a problem, or cured a disease.

Traveling Light

Brag About That!

Don't praise yourself. Let someone else do it.

PROVERBS 27:2

 Demanding respect is like chasing a butterfly. Chase it, and you'll never catch it. Sit still, and it may light on your shoulder. The French philosopher Blaise Pascal asked, "Do you wish people to speak well of you? Then never speak well of yourself." Maybe that's why the Bible says, "Don't praise yourself. Let someone else do it."

Do you feel a need for affirmation? Does your self-esteem need attention? You don't need to drop names or show off. You need only pause at the base of the cross and be reminded of this: The maker of the stars would rather die for you than live without you. And that is a fact. So if you need to brag, brag about that.

Traveling Light

"Come to Me"

"Come to me, all of you who are tired and have heavy loads, and I will give you rest."

Come to me. . . . The invitation is to come to him. Why him?

He offers the invitation as a penniless rabbi in an oppressed nation. He has no political office, no connections with the authorities in Rome. He hasn't written a best-seller or earned a diploma.

Yet, he dares to look into the leathery faces of farmers and tired faces of housewives and offer rest. He looks into the disillusioned eyes of a preacher or two from Jerusalem. He gazes into the cynical stare of a banker and the hungry eyes of a bartender and makes this paradoxical promise: "Take my yoke upon you and learn from me, for I am gentle and humble in heart, and you will find rest for your souls" (Matt. 11:29).

The people came. They came out of the cul-de-sacs and office complexes of their day. They brought him the burdens of their existence, and he gave them not religion, not doctrine, not systems, but rest.

Six Hours One Friday

Jesus Knows

"I am the one God chose and sent into the world."

God with us.

He knows hurt. His siblings called him crazy.

He knows hunger. He made a meal out of wheat-field grains.

He knows exhaustion. So sleepy, he dozed in a storm-tossed boat.

Most of all, he knows sin. Not his own, mind you. But he knows yours.

Every lie you've told.

Person you've hurt.

Promise you've broken.

Every deed you've committed against God— for all sin is against God—Jesus knows. He knows them better than you do. He knows their price. Because he paid it.

Cure for the Common Life

The Embers of Love

God has given us the
Holy Spirit, who fills our hearts with his love.

ROMANS 5:5 CEV

What if you're married to someone you don't love—or who doesn't love you? Many choose to leave. That may be the step you take. But if it is, take at least a thousand others first. And bathe every one of those steps in prayer. Love is a fruit of the Spirit. Ask God to help you love as he loves. "God has given us the Holy Spirit, who fills our hearts with his love." Ask everyone you know to pray for you. Your friends. Your family. Your church leaders. Get your name on every prayer list available. And, most of all, pray for and, if possible, with your spouse. Ask the same God who raised the dead to resurrect the embers of your love. . . .

Isn't it good to know that even when we don't love with a perfect love, he does? God always nourishes what is right. He always applauds what is right. He has never done wrong, led one person to do wrong, or rejoiced when anyone did wrong. For he is love.

A Love Worth Giving

"No More"

*The Lord himself will come
down from heaven with a loud command.*

1 THESSALONIANS 4:16

Have you ever wondered what that command will be? It will be the inaugural word of heaven. It will be the first audible message most have heard from God. It will be the word that closes one age and opens a new one.

I think I know what the command will be. I could very well be wrong, but I think the command that puts an end to the pains of the earth and initiates the joys of heaven will be two words: "No more."

The King of kings will raise his pierced hand and proclaim, "No more."

The angels will stand and the Father will speak, "No more."

Every person who lives and who ever lived will turn toward the sky and hear God announce, "No more."

No more loneliness.

No more tears.

No more death. No more sadness. No more crying. No more pain.

And the Angels Were Silent

Give Up Your Life

He gave up his place with God and made himself nothing.

PHILIPPIANS 2:7

God grants us an uncommon life to the degree we surrender our common one. "If you try to keep your life for yourself, you will lose it. But if you give up your life for me, you will find true life" (Matt. 16:25 NLT).

Jesus did. He "made Himself of no reputation, taking the form of a bondservant, and coming in the likeness of men. . . . He humbled Himself and became obedient to the point of death" (Phil. 2:7–8).

No one in Nazareth saluted him as the Son of God. He did not stand out in his elementary-classroom photograph, demanded no glossy page in his high school annual. Friends knew him as a woodworker, not star hanger. His looks turned no heads; his position earned him no credit. "He gave up his place with God and made himself nothing."

God hunts for those who will do likewise— people through whom he can deliver Christ into the world.

Cure for the Common Life

Words of Hope

Everything that was written in the past was written to teach us, so that . . . we might have hope.

ROMANS 15:4 NIV

 Encourage those who are struggling. Don't know what to say? Then open your Bible. . . .

To the grief stricken: "God has said, 'Never will I leave you; never will I forsake you'" (Heb. 13:5 NIV).

To the guilt ridden: "There is now no condemnation for those who are in Christ Jesus" (Rom. 8:1 NIV).

To the jobless: "In all things God works for the good of those who love him" (Rom. 8:28 NIV).

To those who feel beyond God's grace: "Whoever believes in him shall not perish but have eternal life" (John 3:16 NIV).

Your Bible is a basket of blessings. Won't you share one?

A Love Worth Giving

Choose Love

Those who live in love live in God.

1 JOHN 4:16

From the file entitled "It Ain't Gonna Happen," I pull and pose this suggestion. Let's make Christ's command a federal law. Everyone has to make God's love his or her home. Let it herewith be stated and hereby declared:

> *No person may walk out into the world to begin the day until he or she has stood beneath the cross to receive God's love.*

Cabbies. Presidents. Preachers. Tooth pullers and truck drivers. All required to linger at the fountain of his favor until all thirst is gone.

Don't you ache for the change we'd see? Less honking and locking horns, more hugging and helping kids. We'd pass fewer judgments and more compliments. Forgiveness would skyrocket.

Wild idea? I agree. God's love can't be legislated, but it can be chosen. Choose it, won't you? For Christ's sake, and yours, choose it.

Come Thirsty

Work Can Be Worship

*Everything you do or say
should be done to obey Jesus your Lord.*

COLOSSIANS 3:17

Have you seen the painting *The Angelus*
by Jean-Francois Millet? It portrays two
peasants praying in their field. A church steeple
sits on the horizon, and a light falls from heaven.
The rays do not fall on the church, however.
They don't fall on the bowed heads of the man
and woman. The rays of the sun fall on the
wheelbarrow and the pitchfork at the couple's feet.

God's eyes fall on the work of our hands.
Our Wednesdays matter to him as much as our
Sundays. He blurs the secular and sacred. One
stay-at-home mom keeps this sign over her
kitchen sink: "Divine tasks performed here, daily."
An executive hung this plaque in her office:
"My desk is my altar." Both are correct. With God,
our work matters as much as our worship. Indeed,
work can be worship.

Cure for the Common Life

Life Is Long Enough

*All the days planned for me were
written in your book before I was one day old.*

PSALM 139:16

No person lives one day more or less than God intends. "All the days planned for me were written in your book before I was one day old."

But her days here were so few . . .

His life was so brief . . .

To us it seems that way. We speak of a short life, but compared to eternity, who has a long one? A person's days on earth may appear as a drop in the ocean. Yours and mine may seem like a thimbleful. But compared to the Pacific of eternity, even the years of Methuselah filled no more than a glass. . . .

In God's plan every life is long enough and every death is timely. And though you and I might wish for a longer life, God knows better.

Traveling Light

The Muck and Mire

*God will show his mercy forever and
ever to those who worship and serve him.*

LUKE 1:50

For thirty-three years he would feel
everything you and I have ever felt. He
felt weak. He grew weary. He was afraid of failure.
He was susceptible to wooing women. He got
colds, burped, and had body odor. His feelings
got hurt.

To think of Jesus in such a light is—well,
it seems almost irreverent, doesn't it? It's not
something we like to do; it's uncomfortable. It is
much easier to keep the humanity out of the
incarnation. Clean the manure from around the
manger. Wipe the sweat out of his eyes. Pretend
he never snored or blew his nose or hit his
thumb with a hammer.

He's easier to stomach that way. There is
something about keeping him divine that keeps
him distant, packaged, predictable.

But don't do it. For heaven's sake, don't. Let
him be as human as he intended to be. Let him
into the mire and muck of our world. For only if
we let him in can he pull us out.

God Came Near

November

Those who give up their lives
will save them.

—Luke 17:33

A Love that Never Fails

Love never fails.

1 CORINTHIANS 13:8 NIV

Some of you are so thirsty for this type of love. A love that never fails. Those who should have loved you didn't. Those who could have loved you didn't. You were left at the hospital. Left at the altar. Left with an empty bed. Left with a broken heart. Left with your question "Does anybody love me?"

Please listen to heaven's answer. God loves you. Personally. Powerfully. Passionately. Others have promised and failed. But God has promised and succeeded. He loves you with an unfailing love. And his love—if you will let it—can fill you and leave you with a love worth giving.

So come. Come thirsty and drink deeply.

A Love Worth Giving

God Entered Time

*They will sing about what the LORD has done,
because the LORD's glory is great.*

PSALM 138:5

When God entered time and became a man, he who was boundless became bound. . . . For more than three decades, his once limitless reach would be limited to the stretch of an arm, his speed checked to the pace of human feet.

I wonder, was he ever tempted to reclaim his boundlessness? . . . When the rain chilled his bones, was he tempted to change the weather? When the heat parched his lips, did he give thought to popping over to the Caribbean for some refreshment?

If ever he entertained such thoughts, he never gave in to them. . . . Not once did Christ use his supernatural powers for personal comfort. With one word he could've transformed the hard earth into a soft bed, but he didn't. With a wave of his hand, he could've boomeranged the spit of his accusers back into their faces, but he didn't. With an arch of his brow, he could've paralyzed the hand of the soldier as he braided the crown of thorns. But he didn't.

He Chose the Nails

God Uses the Common

Those who try to keep their lives will lose them.
But those who give up their lives will save them.

LUKE 17:33

Heaven may have a shrine to honor God's
uncommon use of the common.

It's a place you won't want to miss. Stroll
through and see Rahab's rope, Paul's bucket,
David's sling, and Samson's jawbone. Wrap your
hand around the staff that split the sea and smote
the rock. Sniff the ointment that soothed Jesus'
skin and lifted his heart. . . .

I don't know if these items will be there.
But I am sure of one thing—the people who used
them will.

The risk takers: Rahab who sheltered the spy.
The brethren who smuggled Paul.

The conquerors: David, slinging a stone.
Samson, swinging a bone. Moses, lifting a rod.

The caregivers: Mary at Jesus' feet. What she
gave cost much, but somehow she knew what he
would give would cost more.

And the Angels Were Silent

Glimpses of God's Image

*Everything comes from God alone. Everything lives
by his power, and everything is for his glory.*

ROMANS 11:36 TLB

The breath you just took? God gave that.
The blood that just pulsed through your
heart? Credit God. The light by which you read and
the brain with which you process? He gave both.

Everything comes from him . . . and exists
for him. We exist to exhibit God, to display his
glory. We serve as canvases for his brush stroke,
papers for his pen, soil for his seeds, glimpses of
his image.

Cure for the Common Life

Our Ultimate Dilemma

"I am the resurrection and the life.
He who believes in me will live, even though he dies."

JOHN 11:25 NIV

Her words were full of despair. "If you had been here . . ." She stares into the Master's face with confused eyes. She'd been strong long enough; now it hurt too badly. Lazarus was dead. Her brother was gone. And the one man who could have made a difference didn't. He hadn't even made it for the burial. Something about death makes us accuse God of betrayal. "If God were here there would be no death!" we claim.

You see, if God is God anywhere, he has to be God in the face of death. Pop psychology can deal with depression. Pep talks can deal with pessimism. Prosperity can handle hunger. But only God can deal with our ultimate dilemma— death. And only the God of the Bible has dared to stand on the canyon's edge and offer an answer. He has to be God in the face of death. If not, he is not God anywhere.

God Came Near

The Shepherd Leads

He makes me to lie down in green pastures;
He leads me beside the still waters.

PSALM 23:2 NKJV

In the second verse of the Twenty-third Psalm, David the poet becomes David the artist. His quill becomes a brush, his parchment a canvas, and his words paint a picture. A flock of sheep on folded legs, encircling a shepherd. Bellies nestled deep in the long shoots of grass. A still pond on one side, the watching shepherd on the other. "He makes me to lie down in green pastures; He leads me beside the still waters."

Note the two pronouns preceding the two verbs. *He* makes me . . . *He* leads me . . .

Who is the active one? Who is in charge? The shepherd. The shepherd selects the trail and prepares the pasture. The sheep's job—our job— is to watch the Shepherd.

Traveling Light

Courteous Conduct

*Be wise in the way you act
with people who are not believers.*

COLOSSIANS 4:5

Those who don't believe in Jesus note what we do. They make decisions about Christ by watching us. When we are kind, they assume Christ is kind. When we are gracious, they assume Christ is gracious. But if we are brash, what will people think about our King? When we are dishonest, what assumption will an observer make about our Master? No wonder Paul says, "Be wise in the way you act with people who are not believers, making the most of every opportunity. When you talk, you should always be kind and pleasant so you will be able to answer everyone in the way you should" (Col. 4:5–6). Courteous conduct honors Christ.

It also honors his children. When you surrender a parking place to someone, you honor him. When you return a borrowed book, you honor the lender. When you make an effort to greet everyone in the room, especially the ones others may have overlooked, you honor God's children.

A Love Worth Giving

In the Beginning . . .

*"In him there was life,
and that life was the light of all people."*

I've always perceived the apostle John as a fellow who viewed life simply. "Right is right and wrong is wrong, and things aren't nearly as complicated as we make them out to be."

For example, defining Jesus would be a challenge to the best of writers, but John handles the task with casual analogy. The Messiah, in a word, was "the Word." A walking message. A love letter. Be he a fiery verb or a tender adjective, he was, quite simply, a word.

And life? Well, life is divided into two sections, light and darkness. If you are in one, you are not in the other and vice versa.

Next question?

No Wonder They Call Him the Savior

It's Not Up to You

The Spirit speaks to God for
his people in the way God wants.

ROMANS 8:27

None of us pray as much as we should, but all of us pray more than we think, because the Holy Spirit turns our sighs into petitions and tears into entreaties. He speaks for you and protects you. He makes sure you get heard.

Now, suppose a person never . . . learns about the sealing and intercession of the Spirit. This individual thinks that salvation security resides in self, not God, that prayer power depends on the person, not the Spirit. What kind of life will this person lead? A parched and prayerless one.

But what if you believe in the work of the Spirit? Will you be different as a result? You bet your sweet Sunday you will. Your shoulders will lift as you lower the buckling weight of self-salvation. Your knees will bend as you discover the buoyant power of the praying Spirit. Higher walk. Deeper prayers. And, most of all, a quiet confidence that comes from knowing it's not up to you.

Come Thirsty

He Understands

God even knows how many hairs
are on your head. So don't be afraid.

MATTHEW 10:30–31

Why did Jesus grow weary in Samaria
(John 4:6), disturbed in Nazareth (Mark
6:6), and angry in the Temple (John 2:15)?
Why was he sleepy in the boat on the Sea of
Galilee (Mark 4:38), sad at the tomb of Lazarus
(John 11:35), and hungry in the wilderness
(Matt. 4:2)?

Why? Why did he endure all these feelings?
Because he knew you would feel them too.

He knew you would be weary, disturbed,
and angry. He knew you'd be sleepy, grief-stricken,
and hungry. He knew you'd face pain. If not the
pain of the body, the pain of the soul . . . pain too
sharp for any drug. He knew you'd face thirst.
If not a thirst for water, at least a thirst for truth,
and the truth we glean from the image of a thirsty
Christis he understands.

And because he understands, we can come
to him.

He Chose the Nails

Who Does the Saving?

A person is made right with God
through faith, not through obeying the law.

ROMANS 3:28

If we are saved by good works, we don't need God—weekly reminders of the do's and don'ts will get us to heaven. If we are saved by suffering, we certainly don't need God. All we need is a whip and a chain and the gospel of guilt. If we are saved by doctrine then, for heaven's sake, let's study! We don't need God, we need a lexicon.

But be careful, student. For if you are saved by having exact doctrine, then one mistake would be fatal. That goes for those who believe we are made right with God through deeds. I hope the temptation is never greater than the strength. If it is, a bad fall could be a bad omen. And those who think we are saved by suffering, take caution as well, for you never know how much suffering is required.

It took Paul decades to discover what he wrote in only one sentence: "A person is made right with God through faith." Not through good works, suffering, or study.

And the Angels Were Silent

Let Him Change Your Mind

Set your mind on the things above,
not on the things that are on earth.

COLOSSIANS 3:2 NASB

God . . . changes the man by changing the mind. And how does it happen? By . . . considering the glory of Christ. . . .

To behold him is to become like him. As Christ dominates your thoughts, he changes you from one degree of glory to another until—hang on!—you are ready to live with him.

Heaven is the land of sinless minds. . . . Absolute trust. No fear or anger. Shame and second-guessing are practices of a prior life. Heaven will be wonderful, not because the streets are gold, but because our thoughts will be pure.

So what are you waiting on? . . . Give him your best thoughts, and see if he doesn't change your mind.

Next Door Savior

Claim God's Forgiveness

*For as many of you as were
baptized into Christ have put on Christ.*

GALATIANS 3:27 RSV

You read it right. We have "put on" Christ.
When God looks at us he doesn't see us;
he sees Christ. We "wear" him. We are hidden in
him; we are covered by him. As the song says,
"Dressed in his righteousness alone, faultless to
stand before the throne."

Presumptuous, you say? Sacrilegious? It would
be if it were my idea. But it isn't; it's his. We are
presumptuous not when we marvel at his grace,
but when we reject it. And we're sacrilegious not
when we claim his forgiveness, but when we allow
the haunting sins of yesterday to convince us that
God forgives but he doesn't forget.

Do yourself a favor. Remember . . . he forgot.

God Came Near

God With Us

They shall call His name Immanuel,
which is translated, "God with us."

MATTHEW 1:23 NKJV

God's treatment for insignificance won't lead you to a bar or dating service, a spouse or social club. God's ultimate cure for the common life takes you to a manger. The babe of Bethlehem. Immanuel. Remember the promise of the angel? "'Behold, the virgin shall be with child, and bear a Son, and they shall call His name Immanuel,' which is translated, 'God with us'" (Matt. 1:23 NKJV).

Immanuel. The name appears in the same Hebrew form as it did two thousand years ago. "Immanu" means "with us." "El" refers to *Elohim*, or God. Not an "above us God" or a "somewhere in the neighborhood God." He came as the "with us God." God with us.

Not "God with the rich" or "God with the religious." But God with *us*. All of us. Russians, Germans, Buddhists, Mormons, truckdrivers and taxi drivers, librarians. God with *us*.

Cure for the Common Life

The Drama of Redemption

With one sacrifice he made perfect forever
those who are being made holy.

HEBREWS 10:14

We would have scripted the moment differently. Ask us how a God should redeem his world, and we will show you! White horses, flashing swords. Evil flat on his back. God on his throne.

But God on a cross?

A split-lipped, puffy-eyed, blood-masked God on a cross?

Sponge thrust in his face?

Spear plunged in his side?

Dice tossed at his feet?

No, we wouldn't have written the drama of redemption this way. But, then again, we weren't asked to. These players and props were heaven picked and God ordained. We were not asked to design the hour.

But we have been asked to respond to it.

He Chose the Nails

Take Heart!

*May the Lord lead your hearts
into God's love and Christ's patience.*

2 THESSALONIANS 3:5

The majority is not always right. If the majority had ruled, the children of Israel never would have left Egypt. They would have voted to stay in bondage. If the majority had ruled, David never would have fought Goliath. His brothers would have voted for him to stay with the sheep. What's the point? You must listen to your own heart.

God says you're on your way to becoming a disciple when you can keep a clear head and a pure heart.

Do you ever wonder if everything will turn out right as long as you do everything right? Do you ever try to do something right and yet nothing seems to turn out like you planned? Take heart—when people do what is right, God remembers.

The Inspirational Study Bible

Go with Your Heart

After Mary saw Jesus, she went and told his followers,
who were very sad and were crying.

MARK 16:10

Tears represent the heart, the spirit, and the soul of a person. To put a lock and key on your emotions is to bury part of your Christlikeness!

Especially when you come to Calvary.

You can't go to the cross with just your head and not your heart. It doesn't work that way. Calvary is not a mental trip. It's not an intellectual exercise. It's not a divine calculation or a cold theological principle.

It's a heart-splitting hour of emotion.

Don't walk away from it dry-eyed and unstirred. Don't just straighten your tie and clear your throat. Don't allow yourself to descend Calvary cool and collected.

Please . . . pause. Look again.

Those are nails in those hands. That's God on that cross. It's us who put him there.

No Wonder They Call Him the Savior

When Love Is Real

*Rejoice with those who rejoice,
and weep with those who weep.*

ROMANS 12:15 NASB

The summer before my eighth-grade year I made friends with a guy named Larry. He was new to town, so I encouraged him to go out for our school football team. . . .

The result was a good news–bad news scenario. The good news? He made the cut. The bad news? He won my position. I tried to be happy for him, but it was tough.

A few weeks into the season Larry fell off a motorcycle and broke a finger. I remember the day he stood at my front door holding up his bandaged hand. "Looks like you're going to have to play."

I tried to feel sorry for him, but it was hard. The passage was a lot easier for Paul to write than it was for me to practice. "Rejoice with those who rejoice, and weep with those who weep."

You want to plumb the depths of your love for someone? How do you feel when that person succeeds?

A Love Worth Giving

Timely Help

We will find grace to help us when we need it.

HEBREWS 4:16 NLT

God's help is timely. He helps us the same way a father gives plane tickets to his family. When I travel with my kids, I carry all our tickets in my satchel. When the moment comes to board the plane, I stand between the attendant and the child. As each daughter passes, I place a ticket in her hand. She, in turn, gives the ticket to the attendant. Each one receives the ticket in the nick of time.

What I do for my daughters God does for you. He places himself between you and the need. And at the right time, he gives you the ticket. Wasn't this the promise he gave his disciples? "When you are arrested and judged, don't worry ahead of time about what you should say. Say whatever is *given you to say at that time,* because it will not really be you speaking; it will be the Holy Spirit" (Mark 13:11, emphasis mine).

God leads us. He will do the right thing at the right time.

Traveling Light

Do You Doubt?

*Anyone who doubts is like a wave in the sea,
blown up and down by the wind.*

JAMES 1:6

Doubt. He's a nosy neighbor. He's an unwanted visitor. He's an obnoxious guest. He'll pester you. He'll irritate you. He'll criticize your judgment. He'll kick the stool out from under you and refuse to help you up. He'll tell you not to believe in the invisible yet offer no answer for the inadequacy of the visible. . . . His aim is not to convince you but to confuse you. He doesn't offer solutions, he only raises questions.

Had any visits from this fellow lately? If you find yourself going to church in order to be saved and not because you are saved, then you've been listening to him. If you find yourself doubting God could forgive you again for that, you've been sold some snake oil. If you are more cynical about Christians than sincere about Christ, then guess who came to dinner?

I suggest you put a lock on your gate. I suggest you post a "Do Not Enter" sign on your door.

Six Hours One Friday

God Became One of Us

I came to give life—life in all its fullness.

JOHN 10:10

For thousands of years, God gave us his voice. Prior to Bethlehem, he gave his messengers, his teachers, his words. But in the manger, God gave us himself.

Many people have trouble with such a teaching. Islam sees God as one who sends others. He sends angels, prophets, books, but God is too holy to come to us himself. For God to touch the earth would be called a "shirk." People who claim that God has touched the earth shirk God's holiness; they make him gross. They blaspheme him.

Christianity, by contrast, celebrates God's great descent. His nature does not trap him in heaven, but leads him to earth. In God's great gospel, he not only sends, he becomes; he not only looks down, he lives among; he not only talks to us, he lives with us as one of us.

Cure for the Common Life

The Final Gathering

*Always be ready, because you
don't know the day your Lord will come.*

MATTHEW 24:42

Every person who has ever lived will be present at that final gathering. Every heart that has ever beat. Every mouth that has ever spoken. On that day you will be surrounded by a sea of people. Rich, poor. Famous, unknown. Kings, bums. Brilliant, demented. All will be present. And all will be looking in one direction. All will be looking at him. Every human being.

"The Son of Man will come again in his great glory" (Matt. 25:31).

You won't look at anyone else. No side glances to see what others are wearing. No whispers about new jewelry or comments about who is present. At this, the greatest gathering in history, you will have eyes for only one—the Son of Man. Wrapped in splendor. Shot through with radiance. Imploded with light and magnetic in power.

And the Angels Were Silent

The Best Way to Face Life

Teach us how short our lives
really are so that we may be wise.

In a life marked by doctor appointments, dentist appointments, and school appointments, there is one appointment that none of us will miss, the appointment with death. "Everyone must die once, and after that be judged by God" (Heb. 9:27 tev). Oh, how we'd like to change that verse. Just a word or two would suffice. "*Nearly everyone* must die . . ." or "*Everyone but me* must die . . ." or "*Everyone who forgets to eat right and take vitamins* must die . . ." But those are not God's words. In his plan everyone must die, even those who eat right and take their vitamins.

Exercise may buy us a few more heartbeats. Medicine may grant us a few more breaths. But in the end, there is an end. And the best way to face life is to be honest about death.

Traveling Light

Why Did He Do It?

He gave up his place with God and made himself nothing.

PHILIPPIANS 2:7

Holiday travel. It isn't easy. Then why do we do it? Why cram the trunks and endure the airports? You know the answer. We love to be with the ones we love.

The four-year-old running up the sidewalk into the arms of Grandpa.

The cup of coffee with Mom before the rest of the house awakes.

That moment when, for a moment, everyone is quiet as we hold hands around the table and thank God for family and friends and pumpkin pie.

We love to be with the ones we love.

May I remind you? So does God. He loves to be with the ones he loves. How else do you explain what he did? Between him and us there was a distance—a great span. And he couldn't bear it. He couldn't stand it. So he did something about it.

"He gave up his place with God and made himself nothing."

Next Door Savior

A Useful Vessel

"If you give up your life for me, you will find true life."

MATTHEW 16:25 NLT

When you're full of yourself, God can't fill you.

But when you empty yourself, God has a useful vessel. Your Bible overflows with examples of those who did.

In his gospel, Matthew mentions his own name only twice. Both times he calls himself a tax collector. In his list of apostles, he assigns himself the eighth spot.

John doesn't even mention his name in his gospel. The twenty appearances of "John" all refer to the Baptist. John the apostle simply calls himself "the other disciple" or the "disciple whom Jesus loved."

Luke wrote two of the most important books in the Bible but never once penned his own name.

Cure for the Common Life

A Plea for Mercy

The Lord is not . . . willing that any
should perish but that all should come to repentance.

2 PETER 3:9 NKJV

What of those who die with no faith? My husband never prayed. My grandpa never worshiped. My mother never opened a Bible, much less her heart. What about the one who never believed?

How do we know he didn't?

Who among us is privy to a person's final thoughts? Who among us knows what transpires in those final moments? Are you sure no prayer was offered? Eternity can bend the proudest knees. Could a person stare into the yawning canyon of death without whispering a plea for mercy? And could our God, who is partial to the humble, resist it?

He couldn't on Calvary. The confession of the thief on the cross was both a first and final one. But Christ heard it. Christ received it. Maybe you never heard your loved one confess Christ, but who's to say Christ didn't?

Traveling Light

He Didn't Quit

He came to that which was his own,
but his own did not receive him.

JOHN 1:11 NIV

Lee Ielpi is a retired firefighter, a New York City firefighter. He gave twenty-six years to the city. But on September 11, 2001, he gave much more. He gave his son. Jonathan Ielpi was a fireman as well. When the Twin Towers fell, he was there.

Firefighters are a loyal clan. When one perishes in the line of duty, the body is left where it is until a firefighter who knows the person can come and quite literally pick it up. Lee made the discovery of his son's body his personal mission. He dug daily with dozens of others at the sixteen-acre graveyard. On Tuesday, December 11, three months after the disaster, his son was found. And Lee was there to carry him out.

The father didn't quit. Why? Because his love for his son was greater than the pain of the search. Can't the same be said about Christ? Why didn't he quit? Because the love for his children was greater than the pain of the journey.

A Love Worth Giving

Descend Into God's Love

I have no one in heaven but you;
I want nothing on earth besides you.

PSALM 73:25

My friend Keith took his wife, Sarah, to Cozumel, Mexico, to celebrate their anniversary. Sarah loves to snorkel. Give her fins, a mask, and a breathing tube, and watch her go deep. Down she swims, searching for the mysteries below.

Keith's idea of snorkeling includes fins, a mask, and a breathing tube, but it also includes a bellyboard. The surface satisfies him.

Sarah, however, convinced him to take the plunge. Forty feet offshore, she shouted for him to paddle out. He did. The two plunged into the water where she showed him a twenty-foot-tall submerged cross. "If I'd had another breath," he confessed, "the sight would have taken it away."

Jesus waves for you to descend and see the same. Forget surface glances. No more sunburned back. Go deep. Take a breath and descend so deeply into his love that you see nothing else.

Come Thirsty

Saying Yes to God's Purpose

*"I must preach the kingdom of God . . .
because for this purpose I have been sent."*

LUKE 4:42–43 NKJV

After Christ's forty-day pause in the wilderness, the people of Capernaum "tried to keep Him from leaving them; but He said to them, 'I must preach the kingdom of God to the other cities also, because for this purpose I have been sent.'"

He resisted the undertow of the people by anchoring to the rock of his purpose: employing his uniqueness to make a big deal out of God everywhere he could.

And aren't you glad he did? Suppose he had heeded the crowd and set up camp in Capernaum, reasoning, "I thought the whole world was my target and the cross my destiny. But the entire town tells me to stay in Capernaum. Could all these people be wrong?"

Yes they could! In defiance of the crowd, Jesus . . . said no to good things so he could say yes to the right thing: his unique call.

Cure for the Common Life

A Fountain of Love

This is what real love is: . . . it is God's love for us
in sending his Son to be the way to take away our sins.

1 JOHN 4:10

You've had enough of human love. Haven't you? Enough guys wooing you with Elvis-impersonator sincerity. Enough tabloids telling you that true love is just a diet away. Enough helium-filled expectations of bosses and parents and pastors. Enough mornings smelling like the mistakes you made while searching for love the night before.

Don't you need a fountain of love that won't run dry? You'll find one on a stone-cropped hill outside Jerusalem's walls where Jesus hangs, cross-nailed and thorn-crowned. When you feel unloved, ascend this mount. Meditate long and hard on heaven's love for you. Both eyes beaten shut, shoulders as raw as ground beef, lips bloody and split. Fists of hair yanked from his beard. Gasps of air escaping his lungs. As you peer into the crimsoned face of heaven's only Son, remember this: "God showed his great love for us by sending Christ to die for us while we were still sinners" (Rom. 5:8).

Come Thirsty

December

Sing praises to the LORD. . . .
Tell the nations what he has done.

—PSALM 9:11

Christmas Every Day

Sing praises to the LORD. . . .
Tell the nations what he has done.

PSALM 9:11

 You have Christmas every day. Your gift bears, not toys and books, but God himself!

His work: on the cross and in the resurrection. As a result, your sin brings no guilt, and the grave brings no fear.

His energy: it's not up to you. You can do all things through Christ, who gives you strength.

His lordship: he is in charge of you and looks out for you.

His love: what can separate you from it?

Who could imagine such gifts? Who could imagine not opening them?

Come Thirsty

A Bouquet of Blessings

He will rejoice over you with gladness,
He will quiet you with His love.

ZEPHANIAH 3:17 NKJV

Suppose you dwell in a high-rise apartment. On the window sill of your room is a solitary daisy. This morning you picked the daisy and pinned it on your lapel.

But as soon as you're out the door, people start picking petals off your daisy. Someone snags your subway seat. Petal picked. You're blamed for the bad report of a coworker. . . . More petals. By the end of the day, you're down to one. . . . You're only one petal-snatching away from a blowup.

What if the scenario was altered slightly? Let's add one character. The kind man in the apartment next door runs a flower shop. Every night on the way home he stops at your place with a fresh bouquet. Because of him, your apartment has a sweet fragrance, and your step has a happy bounce. Let someone mess with your flower, and you've got a basketful to replace it!

God hand-delivers a bouquet to your door every day. Open it! Take them! Then, when rejections come, you won't be left short-petaled.

A Love Worth Giving

Water for the Soul

"If anyone thirsts, let him come to Me and drink."

JOHN 7:37 NKJV

 Are you *anyone?* If so, then step up to the well. You qualify for his water.

All ages are welcome. Both genders invited. No race excluded. Scoundrels. Scamps. Rascals and rubes. All welcome. You don't have to be rich to drink, religious to drink, successful to drink; you simply need to follow the instructions on what—or better, *who*—to drink. Him. In order for Jesus to do what water does, you must let him penetrate your heart. Deep, deep inside.

Internalize him. Ingest him. Welcome him into the inner workings of your life. Let Christ be the water of your soul.

Come Thirsty

God Is Eternal

God is . . . greater than we can understand!
No one knows how old he is.

Scripture says that the number of God's years is unsearchable. We may search out the moment the first wave slapped on a shore or the first star burst in the sky, but we'll never find the first moment when God was God, for there is no moment when God was not God. He has never *not been*, for he is eternal. God is not bound by time.

But when Jesus came to the earth, all this changed. He heard for the first time a phrase never used in heaven: "Your time is up." As a child, he had to leave the Temple because his time was up. As a man, he had to leave Nazareth because his time was up. And as a Savior, he had to die because his time was up. For thirty-three years, the stallion of heaven lived in the corral of time.

He Chose the Nails

Magnify Your Maker

*If anyone ministers, let him do it as with
the ability which God supplies,
that in all things God may be glorified.*

1 PETER 4:11 NKJV

God endows us with gifts so we can make
him known. Period. God endues the
Olympian with speed, the salesman with savvy,
the surgeon with skill. Why? For gold medals,
closed sales, or healed bodies? Only partially.

The big answer is to make a big to-do out of
God. Brandish him. Herald him. "God has given
gifts to each of you from his great variety of
spiritual gifts. Manage them well. . . . Then God
will be given glory" (1 Pet. 4:10–11 NLT).

Live so that "he'll get all the credit as the One
mighty in everything—encores to the end of time.
Oh, yes!" (1 Pet. 4:11 MSG). Exhibit God with
your uniqueness. When you magnify your Maker
with your strengths, when your contribution
enriches God's reputation, your days grow
suddenly sweet.

Cure for the Common Life

The Master Plan

"It was the LORD's will to crush him."

ISAIAH 53:10 NIV

The cross was no accident.

Jesus' death was not the result of a panicking, cosmological engineer. The cross wasn't a tragic surprise. Calvary was not a knee-jerk response to a world plummeting towards destruction. It wasn't a patch-job or a stop-gap measure. The death of the Son of God was anything but an unexpected peril.

No, it was part of a plan. It was a calculated choice. "It was the Lord's will to crush him." The cross was drawn into the original blueprint. It was written into the script. The moment the forbidden fruit touched the lips of Eve, the shadow of a cross appeared on the horizon. And between that moment and the moment the man with the mallet placed the spike against the wrist of God, a master plan was fulfilled.

God Came Near

Deliver Christ to the World

*I work . . . using Christ's great strength
that works so powerfully in me.*

COLOSSIANS 1:29

The virgin birth is more, much more, than a Christmas story; it is a picture of how close Christ will come to you. The first stop on his itinerary was a womb. Where will God go to touch the world? Look deep within Mary for an answer.

Better still, look deep within yourself. What he did with Mary, he offers to us! He issues a Mary-level invitation to all his children. "If you'll let me, I'll move in!" . . .

What is the mystery of the gospel? "Christ in you, the hope of glory" (Col. 1:27 NIV). . . .

Christ grew in Mary until he had to come out. Christ will grow in you until the same occurs. He will come out in your speech, in your actions, in your decisions. Every place you live will be a Bethlehem, and every day you live will be a Christmas. You, like Mary, will deliver Christ into the world.

Next Door Savior

Slow Down and Rest

*Six days you shall labor and do all your work, but the
seventh day is the Sabbath of the Lord your God. In it you
shall do no work: you, nor your son, nor your daughter.*

God knows us so well. He can see the store
owner reading this verse and thinking,
"Somebody needs to work that day. If I can't, my
son will." So God says, *Nor your son.* "Then my
daughter will." *Nor your daughter.* . . . "I guess I'll
have to send my cow to run the store, or maybe
I'll find some stranger to help me." *No,* God says.
*One day of the week you will say no to work and
yes to worship. You will slow and sit down and lie
down and rest.*

Still we object. . . . "What about my grades?"
"I've got my sales quota." We offer up one reason
after another, but God silences them all with a
poignant reminder: "In six days the Lord made
the heavens and the earth, the sea, and all that is
in them, and rested the seventh day." God's
message is plain: "If creation didn't crash when I
rested, it won't crash when you do."

Repeat these words after me: It is not my job
to run the world.

Traveling Light

A Proper Perspective

Do nothing from selfishness or empty conceit,
but with humility of mind regard one
another as more important than yourselves.

PHILIPPIANS 2:3 NASB

At first glance the standard in that verse seems impossible to meet. Nothing? We shouldn't do *anything* for ourselves? No new dress or suit. What about going to school or saving money—couldn't all of these things be considered selfish?

They could, unless we are careful to understand what Paul is saying. The word the apostle uses for *selfishness* shares a root form with the words *strife* and *contentious*. It suggests a self-preoccupation that hurts others. A divisive arrogance. In fact, first-century writers used the word to describe a politician who procured office by illegal manipulation or a harlot who seduced the client, demeaning both herself and him. . . .

Looking after your personal interests is proper life management. Doing so to the exclusion of the rest of the world is selfishness.

A Love Worth Giving

What Friends Do

A friend loves you all the time.

PROVERBS 17:17

One gets the impression that to John, Jesus was above all a loyal companion. Messiah? Yes. Son of God? Indeed. Miracle worker? That, too. But more than anything Jesus was a pal. Someone you could go camping with or bowling with or count the stars with. . . .

Now what do you do with a friend? (Well, that's rather simple too.) You stick by him.

Maybe that is why John is the only one of the twelve who was at the cross. He came to say good bye. By his own admission he hadn't quite put the pieces together yet. But that didn't really matter. As far as he was concerned, his closest friend was in trouble and he came to help.

"Can you take care of my mother?"

Of course. That's what friends are for.

No Wonder They Call Him the Savior

God's Ways Are Right

When you pass through the waters, I will be with you;
and through the rivers, they will not overflow you.

ISAIAH 43:2–3 NASB

 God knows what is best. No struggle will come your way apart from his purpose, presence, and permission. What encouragement this brings! You are never the victim of nature or the prey of fate. Chance is eliminated. You are more than a weather vane whipped about by the winds of fortune. Would God truly abandon you to the whims of drug-crazed thieves, greedy corporate raiders, or evil leaders? Perish the thought!

We live beneath the protective palm of a sovereign King who superintends every circumstance of our lives and delights in doing us good.

Nothing comes your way that has not first passed through the filter of his love.

Come Thirsty

Prophecy Fulfilled

Those who look to the LORD will praise him.

PSALM 22:26

The fulfillment of Scripture is a recurring theme in the passion.

Why, in his final moments, was Jesus determined to fulfill prophecy? He knew we would doubt. He knew we would question. And since he did not want our heads to keep his love from our hearts, he used his final moments to offer proof that he was the Messiah. He systematically fulfilled centuries-old prophecies. . . .

Did you know that in his life Christ fulfilled 332 distinct prophecies in the Old Testament? What are the mathematical possibilities of all these prophecies being fulfilled in the life of one man?

1

840,000,000,000,000,000,000,000,
000,000,000,000,000,000,000,000,
000,000,000,000,000,000,000,000,000,
000,000,000,000,000,000

(That's ninety-seven zeroes!) Amazing!

He Chose the Nails

A Well of Optimism

You must change and become like little children.
Otherwise, you will never enter the kingdom of heaven.

MATTHEW 18:3

Bedtime is a bad time for kids. No child understands the logic of going to bed while there is energy left in the body or hours left in the day.

My children are no exception. A few years ago, after many objections and countless groans, the girls were finally in their gowns, in their beds, and on their pillows. I slipped into the room to give them a final kiss. Andrea, the five-year-old, was still awake, just barely, but awake. After I kissed her, she lifted her eyelids one final time and said, "I can't wait until I wake up."

Oh, for the attitude of a five-year-old! That simple uncluttered passion for living that can't wait for tomorrow. A philosophy of life that reads, "Play hard, laugh hard, and leave the worries to your father." A bottomless well of optimism flooded by a perpetual spring of faith. Is it any wonder Jesus said we must have the heart of a child before we can enter the kingdom of heaven?

And the Angels Were Silent

Facing the Facts

How precious also are Your thoughts to me,
O God! How great is the sum of them!

PSALM 139:17 NKJV

Aging is a universal condition. But the way we try to hide it, you would think it was a plague!

There are girdles which compact the middle-age spread for both sexes. There are hair transplants, wigs, toupees, and hair pieces. Dentures bring youth to the mouth, wrinkle cream brings youth to the face, and color in a bottle brings youth to the hair.

All to hide what everyone already knows—we're getting older. . . .

Just when the truth about life sinks in, God's truth starts to surface. He takes us by the hand and dares us not to sweep the facts under the rug but to confront them with him at our side.

Aging? A necessary process to pass on to a better world.

Death? Merely a brief passage, a tunnel.

Self? Designed and created for a purpose, purchased by God himself.

There, was that so bad?

God Came Near

God Sent Himself

The Word became flesh and dwelt among us.

JOHN 1:14 NKJV

Don't we love the word "with"? "Will you go *with* me?" we ask. "To the store, to the hospital, through my life?" God says he will. "I am *with* you always," Jesus said before he ascended to heaven, "to the very end of the age" (Matt. 28:20 NIV). Search for restrictions on the promise; you'll find none. You won't find "I'll be with you if you behave . . . when you believe. I'll be with you on Sundays in worship . . . at mass." No, none of that. There's no withholding tax on God's "with" promise. He is *with* us.

God is with us.

Prophets weren't enough. Apostles wouldn't do. Angels won't suffice. God sent more than miracles and messages. He sent himself; he sent his Son. "The Word became flesh and dwelt among us."

Cure for the Common Life

What to Do with Worries

> *God did not keep back his own Son,*
> *but he gave him for us. If God*
> *did this, won't he freely give us everything else?*
>
> ROMANS 8:32 CEV

What do we do with . . . worries? Take your anxieties to the cross—literally. Next time you're worried about your health or house or finances or flights, take a mental trip up the hill. Spend a few moments looking again at the pieces of passion.

Run your thumb over the tip of the spear. Balance a spike in the palm of your hand. Read the wooden sign written in your own language. And as you do, touch the velvet dirt, moist with the blood of God.

Blood he bled for you.

The spear he took for you.

The nails he felt for you.

The sign he left for you.

He did all of this for you. Knowing this, knowing all he did for you there, don't you think he'll look out for you here?

He Chose the Nails

God's Love

God is love.

1 JOHN 4:16

The supreme surprise of God's love? It has nothing to do with you. Others love you because of you, because your dimples dip when you smile or your rhetoric charms when you flirt. Some people love you because of you. Not God. He loves you because he is he. He loves you because he decides to. Self-generated, uncaused, and spontaneous, his constant-level love depends on his choice to give it. "The LORD did not set his affection on you and choose you because you were more numerous than other peoples, for you were the fewest of all peoples. But it was because the LORD loved you" (Deut. 7:7–8 NIV).

You don't influence God's love. You can't impact the treeness of a tree, the skyness of the sky, or the rockness of a rock. Nor can you affect the love of God.

Come Thirsty

God Uses People

Happy are those who are helped by the God of Jacob.

PSALM 146:5

Until he was eighty years old he looked like he wouldn't amount to much more than a once-upon-a-time prince turned outlaw. Would you choose a wanted murderer to lead a nation out of bondage? Would you call upon a fugitive to carry the Ten Commandments? God did. And he called him, of all places, right out of the sheep pasture. Called his name through a burning bush. Scared old Moses right out of his shoes! There, with knees knocking and "Who me?" written all over his face, Moses agreed to go back into the ring. . . .

The reassuring lesson is clear. God used (and uses!) people to change the world. People! Not saints or superhumans or geniuses, but people. Crooks, creeps, lovers, and liars—he uses them all. And what they may lack in perfection, God makes up for in love.

No Wonder They Call Him the Savior

When the Time Comes

*God will help you deal with whatever
hard things come up when the time comes.*

MATTHEW 6:34 MSG

That last phrase is worthy of your highlighter: "when the time comes."

"I don't know what I'll do if my husband dies." You will, *when the time comes.*

"When my children leave the house, I don't think I can take it." It won't be easy, but strength will arrive *when the time comes.*

"I could never lead a church. There is too much I don't know." You may be right. Or you may be wanting to know everything too soon. Could it be that God will reveal answers to you *when the time comes?*

The key is this: Meet today's problems with today's strength. Don't start tackling tomorrow's problems until tomorrow. You do not have tomorrow's strength yet. You simply have enough for today.

Traveling Light

Made By the Master

You knit me together in my mother's womb.

PSALM 139:13 NIV

"Knitted together" is how the psalmist described the process of God making man. Not manufactured or mass-produced, but knitted. Each thread of personality tenderly intertwined. Each string of temperament deliberately selected.

God as creator. Pensive. Excited. Inventive.

An artist, brush on pallet, seeking the perfect shade.

A composer, fingers on keyboard, listening for the exact chord.

A poet, pen poised on paper, awaiting the precise word.

The Creator, the master weaver, threading together the soul.

Each one different. No two alike. None identical.

Six Hours One Friday

Gifted to Give

A spiritual gift is given to each of us
as a means of helping the entire church.

1 CORINTHIANS 12:7 NLT

When you place your trust in Christ, he places his Spirit in you. And when the Spirit comes, he brings gifts, housewarming gifts of sorts. "A spiritual gift is given to each of us as a means of helping the entire church" (1 Cor. 12:7 NLT). Remember, God prepacked you with strengths. When you become a child of God, the Holy Spirit requisitions your abilities for the expansion of God's kingdom, and they become spiritual gifts. The Holy Spirit may add other gifts according to his plan. But no one is gift deprived.

Lonely? God is with you.

Depleted? He funds the overdrawn.

Weary of an ordinary existence? Your spiritual adventure awaits.

The cure for the common life begins and ends with God.

Cure for the Common Life

A Leaf of Hope

When the dove returned to [Noah] in the evening,
there in its beak was a freshly plucked olive leaf!

GENESIS 8:11 NIV

An olive leaf. Noah would have been happy to have the bird but to have the leaf! This leaf was more than foliage; this was promise. The bird brought more than a piece of a tree; it brought hope. For isn't that what hope is? Hope is an olive leaf—evidence of dry land after a flood. . . .

Don't we love the olive leaves of life? "It appears the cancer may be in remission." "I can help you with those finances." "We'll get through this together."

What's more, don't we love the doves that bring them? When the father walks his son through his first broken heart, he gives him an olive leaf. When the wife of many years consoles the wife of a few months, when she tells her that conflicts come and all husbands are moody and these storms pass, you know what she is doing? She is giving an olive leaf.

We love olive leaves. And we love those who give them.

A Love Worth Giving

Love that Lasts Forever

Love never fails.

1 CORINTHIANS 13:8 NIV

"Love," Paul says, "never fails."

The verb Paul uses for the word *fail* is used elsewhere to describe the demise of a flower as it falls to the ground, withers, and decays. It carries the meaning of death and abolishment. God's love, says the apostle, will never fall to the ground, wither, and decay. By its nature, it is permanent. It is never abolished.

Love "will last forever" (NLT).

It "never dies" (MSG).

It "never ends" (RSV).

Love "is eternal" (TEV).

God's love "will never come to an end" (NEB). . . .

Governments will fail, but God's love will last. Crowns are temporary, but love is eternal. Your money will run out, but his love never will.

A Love Worth Giving

His Name Is Jesus

> *Joseph . . . took to him his wife, and*
> *did not know her till she had brought forth*
> *her firstborn Son. And he called His name Jesus.*
>
> MATTHEW 1:24–25 NKJV

Joseph tanked his reputation. He swapped his *tsadiq* diploma for a pregnant fiancée and an illegitimate son and made the big decision of discipleship. He placed God's plan ahead of his own.

Rather than make a name for himself, he made a home for Christ. And because he did, a great reward came his way. "He called His name Jesus."

Queue up the millions who have spoken the name of Jesus, and look at the person selected to stand at the front of the line. Joseph. Of all the saints, sinners, prodigals, and preachers who have spoken the name, Joseph, a blue-collar, small-town construction worker said it first. He cradled the wrinkle-faced prince of heaven and with an audience of angels and pigs, whispered, "Jesus . . . You'll be called Jesus."

Cure for the Common Life

God Came Near

His kingdom will never end.

LUKE 1:33

She looks into the face of the baby. Her son. Her Lord. His Majesty. At this point in history, the human being who best understands who God is and what he is doing is a teenage girl in a smelly stable. She can't take her eyes off him. Somehow Mary knows she is holding God. So this is he. She remembers the words of the angel. "His kingdom will never end."

He looks like anything but a king. His face is prunish and red. His cry, though strong and healthy, is still the helpless and piercing cry of a baby. And he is absolutely dependent upon Mary for his well-being.

Majesty in the midst of the mundane. Holiness in the filth of sheep manure and sweat. Divinity entering the world on the floor of a stable, through the womb of a teenager and in the presence of a carpenter.

She touches the face of the infant-God.

God Came Near

Facing Fear

> *"Father, if you are willing,*
> *take away this cup of suffering."*
>
> LUKE 22:42

Jesus was more than anxious; he was afraid. . . .

How remarkable that Jesus felt such fear. But how kind that he told us about it. We tend to do the opposite. Gloss over our fears. Cover them up. Keep our sweaty palms in our pockets, our nausea and dry mouths a secret. Not so with Jesus. We see no mask of strength. But we do hear a request for strength.

"Father, if you are willing, take away this cup of suffering." The first one to hear his fear is his Father. He could have gone to his mother. He could have confided in his disciples. He could have assembled a prayer meeting. All would have been appropriate, but none were his priority. He went first to his Father.

Traveling Light

A Free Choice

God did not choose us to suffer his anger
but to have salvation through our Lord Jesus Christ.

1 THESSALONIANS 5:9

We don't like to talk about hell, do we?

In intellectual circles the topic of hell is regarded as primitive and foolish. It's not logical. "A loving God wouldn't send people to hell." So we dismiss it.

But to dismiss it is to dismiss a core teaching of Jesus. The doctrine of hell is not one developed by Paul, Peter, or John. It is taught by Jesus himself.

And to dismiss it is to dismiss much more. It is to dismiss the presence of a loving God and the privilege of a free choice. Let me explain.

We are free either to love God or not. He invites us to love him. He urges us to love him. He came that we might love him. But, in the end, the choice is yours and mine. To take that choice from each of us, for him to force us to love him, would be less than love.

God explains the benefits, outlines the promises, and articulates very clearly the consequences. And then, in the end, he leaves the choice to us.

And the Angels Were Silent

A Tiny Seed, a Tiny Deed

Do not despise . . . small beginnings,
for the LORD rejoices to see the work begin.

ZECHARIAH 4:10 NLT

Against a towering giant, a brook pebble seems futile. But God used it to topple Goliath. Compared to the tithes of the wealthy, a widow's coins seem puny. But Jesus used them to inspire us. . . .

Moses had a staff.
David had a sling.
Samson had a jawbone.
Rahab had a string.
Mary had some ointment.
Dorcas had a needle.
All were used by God.
What do you have?
God inhabits the tiny seed, empowers the tiny deed. . . . Don't discount the smallness of your deeds.

Cure for the Common Life

Homesick for Heaven

Our homeland is in heaven.

PHILIPPIANS 3:20

This home we're in won't last forever.
Birthdays remind us of that.

Not long ago I turned fifty. I'm closer to ninety than I am to infancy. All those things they say about aging are coming true. I'm patting myself less on the back and more under the chin. I have everything I had twenty years ago, except now it's all lower. The other day I tried to straighten out the wrinkles in my socks and found out I wasn't wearing any.

Aging. It's no fun. The way we try to avoid it, you'd think we could. We paint the body, preserve the body, protect the body. And well we should. These bodies are God's gifts. We should be responsible. But we should also be realistic. This body must die so the new body can live. "Flesh and blood cannot have a part in the kingdom of God. Something that will ruin cannot have a part in something that never ruins" (1 Cor. 15:50).

Traveling Light

The God Who Follows

The upright shall dwell in Your presence.

PSALM 140:14 NKJV

Lazarus was three days dead in a sealed tomb when he heard a voice, lifted his head, and looked over his shoulder and saw Jesus standing. God had followed him into death.

Peter had denied his Lord and gone back to fishing when he heard his name and looked over his shoulder and saw Jesus cooking breakfast. God had followed him in spite of his failure.

God is the God who follows. I wonder . . . have you sensed him following you? We often miss him. . . . But he comes.

Through the kindness of a stranger. The majesty of a sunset. The mystery of romance. Through the question of a child or the commitment of a spouse. Through a word well spoken or a touch well timed, have you sensed his presence?

Traveling Light

Our Sure God

*Surely goodness and mercy shall follow me
all the days of my life; and I will
dwell in the house of the LORD forever.*

PSALM 23:6 NKJV

Look at the first word: *surely*. David didn't
say, "*Maybe* goodness and mercy shall
follow me." Or "*Possibly* goodness and mercy
shall follow me." Or "*I have a hunch* that goodness
and mercy shall follow me." David could have used
one of those phrases. But he didn't. He believed in
a sure God, who makes sure promises and provides
a sure foundation. David would have loved
the words of one of his great-great-grandsons, the
apostle James. He described God as the one "with
whom there is never the slightest variation or
shadow of inconsistency" (James 1:17 PHILLIPS).

Our moods may shift, but God's doesn't.
Our minds may change, but God's doesn't. Our
devotion may falter, but God's never does. Even if
we are faithless, he is faithful, for he cannot betray
himself (2 Tim. 2:13). He is a sure God.

Traveling Light

ACKNOWLEDGEMENTS

Grateful acknowledgment is made to the following publishers for permission to reprint this copyrighted material. All copyrights are held by the author, Max Lucado.

Lucado, Max. *And the Angels Were Silent* (Nashville: W Publishing Group, 2003).

———*Come Thirsty* (Nashville: W Publishing Group, 2004).

———*Cure for the Common Life* (Nashville: W Publishing Group, 2005).

———*He Chose the Nails* (Nashville: W Publishing Group, 2000).

———General Editor, *The Inspirational Study Bible* (Nashville: W Publishing Group, 1995)

———*God Came Near* (Nashville: W Publishing Group, 2003).

———*A Love Worth Giving* (Nashville: W Publishing Group, 2002).

———*Next Door Savior* (Nashville: W Publishing Group, 2003).

———*No Wonder They Call Him the Savior* (Nashville: W Publishing Group, 2003).

———*Six Hours One Friday* (Nashville: W Publishing Group, 2003).

———*Traveling Light* (Nashville: W Publishing Group, 2000).

Visit the all new
www.graceforthemoment.com and
sign up to receive a free
"Grace Thought" from Max Lucado
in your e-mail box every week.

We are all unique individuals, created in God's image, with our own gifts, strengths and passions. In his winsome, encouraging voice, Max will give readers practical tools for exploring and identifying our own uniqueness, motivation to put our uniqueness to work and perspective to redefine our concept of work. It's never too late to uncover your strengths, discover God's will or redirect your career, in this great product line,

Cure for the Common Life

www.maxlucado.com

Book ISBN: 0849900085
Workbook ISBN: 14818506052

CD ISBN: 0849963818
Spanish ed. ISBN: 0881139025

CARIBE-BETANIA EDITORES
A Division of Thomas Nelson Publishers
Since 1798

NELSON IMPACT
A Division of Thomas Nelson Publishers
Since 1798

W PUBLISHING GROUP
A Division of Thomas Nelson Publishers
Since 1798